108
Beloved Objects

Letting Go of Stuff, Keeping Our Stories

108 Beloved Objects

Letting Go of Stuff, Keeping Our Stories

Jeff Greenwald

Copyright © 2021 by Jeff Greenwald

Several stories in this book have previously appeared in *Hidden Compass*, *Foreign Literary*, and *Perceptive Travel*.

All object photographs on neutral backgrounds © 2021 by Zena Kruzick. Photographer of burning memorial on page 234 unknown. Illustration on page 158 from cancer.gov website. Author photo by Bobby Lee. All other images © 2021 by Jeff Greenwald.

108 Beloved Objects: Letting Go of Stuff, Keeping Our Stories

Author: Jeff Greenwald

Designer: Colleen Shelley

Paperback: 978-1-7347918-6-0

Engage with the book and its objects online at 108Objects.com

To Life

Table of Contents

INTRODUCTION..1

TRAVEL..8

GIFTS..46

EARTH, MOON & STARS..................................84

LOVE...122

ENDINGS...160

SPIRIT..199

AFTERWORD...237

ACKNOWLEDGMENTS....................................239

Introduction

In *Reflections on the Art of Living*, Joseph Campbell talks about a ritual he attended in a Kentucky forest. Forty-nine people were asked to bring seven small, symbolic objects representing "seven things for which your life is worth living."

The people—divided into seven groups of seven—entered the mouth of a cave. As the ritual progressed, each person was asked to give up one thing after another until, by the end, they left the cavern with the one thing they most cherished in this life. "And you found out what it was, believe me," writes Campbell, "and the order in which you gave up your treasures was revelatory: you really knew what your order of values was."

One hundred and eight objects is a lot more than seven, but even that number represents only a fraction of the stuff I've acquired during my life. I don't mean "stuff" like sports jackets or serving bowls, my car or motorcycle; I'm talking about things that encapsulate a moment in my life. Sometimes a single object—like a book of matches—is enough to bring back the smell of a jazz club in Hong Kong; a black stone can conjure a holy mountain. Like our genetic maps, such objects decode the priorities and attachments that have shaped who we are.

Campbell's lesson is valuable to us all. We share an immutable truth: Eventually, we really *do* have to give up everything. Rarely do we get a choice to do so in any sort of meaningful order, or even with full awareness of the process. If we could, it's not difficult to imagine what those last few things—the ones we would choose to hold onto until our last breath—might be. None of them, in most cases, will be objects: our self-awareness; our time with those we love; our ability to experience pleasure; a beloved pet; a spell among the redwood giants or under the winter stars.

But give them up we will. Everything must go. Our objects, in truth, will not be the most difficult things to part with.

*　*　*

Our strangely codependent relationship (and inevitable breakup) with our beloved belongings has been on my mind since 2010, when my friend Sandy recruited me for a part-time job. I was hired to help dissolve a major San Francisco law firm that, after 85 years, had declared bankruptcy. My mission was to catalogue the thousands of case files the firm had accumulated over the decades, and ship them back to their respective attorneys. (At their expense, of course.)

The law offices took up two entire floors of a skyscraper on 2nd Street. When the firm collapsed, the stunned employees—from actuaries to secretaries—were given 15 minutes to vacate the premises. Our small wrap-up crew had a suite of bare-bones cubicles on a corner of the otherwise empty first floor.

One afternoon, Sandy (who'd been with the company 15 years) brought me up to the second floor. Though still leased by the law firm, it seemed occupied only by ghosts. All the trappings of an active office were still in place—except for people. It was eerie, almost chilling. The scene recalled the *Marie Celeste*, a merchant ship found abandoned at sea in 1872, burl pipes still smoldering in the ashtrays.

"Look around," Sandy said, motioning across the vast abandoned space. "You can keep anything you find."

Though we were the only people on the second floor, many reminders of a human presence remained. Bowls of Hershey's Kisses and tins of Altoids mints sat on metal desks; cubicle walls were tacked with preschoolers' drawings, Mother's Day cards, and vacation photos. Stuffed koalas and plastic penguins formed lonely menageries atop boxy computer speakers. Inside the desk drawers, crowded in with pens and paper clips, lay flashlights and key rings, rabbits' feet and souvenir letter openers, fancy pens, whiskey flasks, even a small brass kaleidoscope.

Each one of these items had meant something. They'd been part of the tapestry of someone's life—reminders of intimate connections, small victories, moments of delight. They were sentimental links to an existence beyond the cubicle walls, antidotes to an environment founded on predatory success. From ceramic mugs celebrating The World's Best Dad to snow globes from St. Louis, every object was like a fingerprint: the trace of a life contained, but not defined, by these offices.

Introduction

I stopped in front of an antiqued globe on a hardwood stand. A small brass plaque on the base honored a "Secretary of the Year."

"Take it," Sandy shrugged. "Take anything. Whatever you want. Because at some point—any day now—we'll lose our lease on this floor."

"Why?"

"For nonpayment of rent."

"And then...? What happens to all this stuff?"

"It gets tossed into a dumpster."

From that day on, every lunch break was a scavenger hunt. As awkward as it felt to comb these chambers and rifle through the desks, it was a legal endeavor: If a ship is abandoned, any objects thrown overboard are free to claim. They are jetsam, subject to the law of the briny deep. So when I found an item of value—a lumbar cushion, a Swiss Army knife, a case of microwave popcorn—it was an act of recovery, rather than looting.

My job lasted only a few more months before our operation was shuttered, and the offices gutted to make way for a tech start-up. By that point, I'd stopped raiding the second floor. But though my salvage expeditions had ended, the experience opened a window onto my own life.

Someday, I realized, I'll be "shuttered" as well. When that happens, my treasures may share the same fate as those koalas and kaleidoscopes.

* * *

After my gig at the law firm, I began to see my own possessions in a new light. Looking around my Oakland flat (which I've inhabited for more than 30 years), I realized how many of the objects I've accumulated—each one the signature of an indelible adventure, encounter, or passage in my life—had become nearly invisible. The vibrancy they once possessed had faded into the cosmic background radiation of my universe.

For many people, such a collection of keepsakes has a future destination. Their spouse, kids, or grandchildren will take possession of it, and spend a few weekends of their time ferreting out items of sentimental or utilitarian value before hauling the remaining detritus to Goodwill.

Not me. There are no beneficiaries for my stuff. I'm not married. My godchildren aren't interested. And I don't wish to saddle my executors with the task of dealing with an apartment full of the personally priceless but objectively worthless trinkets I've amassed during four decades of travel, journalism, and serial monogamy.

These objects meant a great deal when I acquired them: a brass faucet from a Cambodian refugee camp, a small oil painting from Kazakhstan, a beaker from my father's darkroom. There are scores of these mementos, and they are everywhere. It is impossible to wander through my bathroom, bedroom, or kitchen without encountering a once-beloved object. To free some space for myself as I play out the last act of this lifetime, I'd like to clear away as many of them as possible.

Confronting a plethora of possessions can be a daunting task. Fortunately, I have a mild personality disorder that often serves me well. Somewhat obsessive-compulsive, I find it far easier to deal with things if they are numbered. After a dinner party, for example. I cannot cope with a full sink, so I make a deal with myself: I will wash 47 dishes. Planning out my week, I'll list as many to-dos as will fit onto a single page of a 4x6 notepad. If my apartment is messy, I'll pick an arbitrary number (say, 24) and file away exactly that many books, bills, and magazines. It's a little bit crazy. But it makes it possible for me to get things done.

And so I decided that, to make my de-cluttering manageable, I would commit to relinquishing exactly 108 objects from my delightful but cluttered world. And in gathering the 108 objects for this book, I've grouped them into six realms: *Travel; Gifts; Earth, Moon, and Stars; Love; Endings; Spirit*. Each realm is preceded by a brief introduction, recalling one object that encapsulates, for me, the strange enchantment that sphere has cast on my life.

* * *

Almost everyone who hears about this project asks: Why specifically *108 objects*? Well, the number is deeply significant in Eastern spiritual practice, and beyond. It is the number of prayer beads on a *malla* (a Buddhist rosary), and the number of yoga postures in a full cycle. The number 18 means chai, or "life," in Hebrew numerology. Multiples of this number in money—e.g., six times $18 is $108—are given as gifts at bar mitzvahs and Jewish weddings. Also, it so happens, there are 108 stitches on a baseball. And on a personal note, I'd like to live through 1,008 full moons by the reachable age, in today's world, of 84.

My initial strategy was to simply dispose of these 108 items. I'd count them out and carry them to the curb, where they'd be taken by passersby. But as I began to actually gather these objects, I understood that they would not be abandoned lightly. Some hold value not so much for what they are (a blue yo-yo, a bundle of cotton wicks), but for the people and places they recall—and the states of nostalgia they reawaken.

Introduction

Each object still radiates significance. Each recalls a fragment of my world. Like the tattered protagonists of *Toy Story*, each object has a tale to tell, and resists the insult of being discarded.

There is an emerging field in biology called biosemiotics. It's a controversial theory which holds that all evolution, all of life on every level, is steered by the recognition of (and response to) signs and codes. Looking at my objects one by one, the theory makes sense. The ones I've held onto are valuable mainly as symbols: devices to trigger my memory. On a biosemiotic level, each is a key that unlocks my hippocampus. The cash value of each object is its story.

And telling stories is what a traveler does—whether in print, over a pint, or (as in my case) on the stage.

Since 2003, I've been performing a solo show called *Strange Travel Suggestions*. The name was inspired, of course, by that famous line from Kurt Vonnegut Jr.'s *Cat's Cradle*: "Peculiar travel suggestions," he wrote, "are dancing lessons from God." I fully agree. When we travel at our best we are like that Fool in the tarot deck, filled with youthful confidence, making a leap of faith into the universe. The unexpected places we visit, the people we spontaneously befriend, the "strange travel suggestions" we accept, shape the destiny of our travels—and sometimes, our lives.

My show is interactive. Volunteers from the audience are called to the stage, where they spin a large, colorful "Wheel of Fortune." Mesmerizing under the spotlights, the wheel is ringed by 30 strange glyphs and symbols. The 30 stops don't stand for specific stories or places. They represent themes: The Celestial Sphere. The Fool. Unexpected Gifts. Depending on where the wheel stops, a story on that theme—taken from my lifetime of travel—is told. Neither I nor the audience knows where the night will take us. Each show is a journey into the unknown— a spontaneous expedition that unfolds as it progresses, with different destinations every time.

Since only a limited number of people can attend these shows (and none, at present), I've often been asked if I might adapt my show for the page. *108 Beloved Objects* is an attempt to do just that. This is a work of "flash nonfiction," in which every object evokes a short tale. It can be read in sequence, or in any order at all.

* * *

By this point you might be asking yourself a question. I had the same thought: If I'm "letting go" of all of this stuff, where is it going?

As I prepare to relinquish these objects, I'm sharing the stories attached to them. The objects themselves will be given to my readers, both here and on the *108Objects.com* website. So drop me a line. Let me know if one of these objects speaks to you, and why. Make a good case, and (for only the cost of postage) I'll send it to you.

It's my hope that, in this way, many (if not all) of these beloved objects will find new homes.

I'm not the first person to do something in this vein. From ancient Vedic mendicants to the traditional potlatch feasts of the Pacific Northwest tribes, from the Museum of Broken Relationships in Zagreb to Marie Kondo's clutter-busting *The Life-Changing Magic of Tidying Up* and Roz Chast's wonderful *Can't We Talk About Something More Pleasant?*, there have been innumerable tales of people parting with things they love but no longer need. We seem to understand, at a deep level, that to release our possessions is a path to personal freedom.

The ironic thing is how difficult it can be. It sometimes seems as if our possessions own *us*; we have that little agency over them. Collecting is easy; letting go, not so much.

In her introduction to *The Museum of Broken Relationships: A Diary*—which has much in common with this project—co-curator Olinka Vištica quotes Mary Oliver's poem "In Blackwater Woods," in which the poet names three things we must do "To live in this world:" To love what is mortal; to hold it; and to let it go.

But moving through this life involves more than letting go. While we're alive on Earth (heaven, hell, or reincarnation to the contrary notwithstanding), our journey consists of passing from one handhold to another. To let go of one thing means embracing something else—ultimately, our own mortality. So even the idea of "letting go" is something we shouldn't hold onto too tightly.

And that's why this experiment will end with naming the three objects I cannot let go of: the objects that, had I been in that Kentucky cave with Joseph Campbell, would have been the last worldly possessions I'd have abandoned.

There are some things I hope to accomplish with this project. I wish to learn what's essential; to leave a record; and to travel forward, from this point on, more lightly.

But nothing summarizes my deepest aspirations more wonderfully than a letter I received from my close friend Kristina, in January 2011: the morning before a 6-week run of "Strange Travel Suggestions" was about to open at The Marsh in San Francisco. I was unsure of my material, worried about stagecraft, and struggling with stage fright. Ever since, I've read her note before every performance.

Introduction

I wish for you to relax as best you can, and open your heart to all the Beauty, Joy, Wisdom, and Silliness in your stories. You are there to move people; to touch their hearts or minds in a way that makes them feel a little more alive than when they showed up: a noble and achievable goal. You are surrounded by kindred spirits—which should give you comfort—and you will create something tonight for them. I hope that you may also be moved as you tap into your soul, and tell the stories of your interesting life and all those you've met. You are a storyteller—and now you get to do the thing you were meant to do. Whatever bumps you might feel, connect with yourself, and tell your stories.

Yes. Thank you. On with the show.

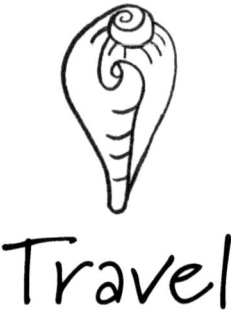

Travel

The objects in this book are like fragments of a hologram, each encapsulating the whole of an ever-expanding portrait. So it was a little difficult, at first, to imagine a single object that might introduce this section—something that brings together the nearly 50 years during which travel has been my passion, and the ridgepole of my life.

But the object of choice seems obvious, actually.

During the course of my life I've held six passports; my current one expires in 2029. But the one I'm leafing through now was issued in 1990, and traveled with me during my land-and-sea circumnavigation of the globe from December 1993 through September 1994. Though we tend to think of a passport as neutral—a kind of catalyst that makes world travel possible, but doesn't figure much into the experience itself—this one is an exception. Time and again, it was a mute witness to some of my most memorable passages.

Leaving Greece, I remember clutching this passport tightly in my hand as I waited at emigration for Alex—a beautiful Canadian artist who had promised to join me on my voyage onward to Istanbul. And how reluctantly I surrendered it to the officials, realizing that she was not going to appear.

Arriving in Mali via a packed, sweltering, overnight train just past midnight, on the 13th of February, 1994, this passport was seized by an immigration officer who looked at the picture and then back at me, incredulous. "Is this your *son*?," he demanded. "No," I sighed. "That was me—before the train."

As I attempted to enter Saudi Arabia during the 1994 *haj* to Mecca, the customs inspector held the passport behind his back, demanding I answer a question before he'd return it to me. "Was Michael Jackson a Negro, or a white man?" It was the riddle of the Sphinx; I pondered long and hard before answering. "He was born a Negro," I replied, "But he will die a white man." The inspector nodded approvingly, and stamped my visa.

And then in Pakistan, arriving at sunset on a cockroach-infested ferry carrying new cars to Karachi from Dubai. I was the only passenger. The five-day trip across the Gulf of Oman had taken seven; by the end, I and the small crew were surviving on root beer and *naan*. I'd spent the week sleeping in a new Toyota van, and—when nature called—clutching a frayed rope while hanging my ass over the wooden rail. At last we arrived. Now it was Friday night, and no sight had ever looked better to me than the skyline of Karachi, with its soft hotel beds and hot showers. The border agent glanced at my passport, then returned it to my hand. "Immigration office closed," he declared. "You must stay on the boat until Monday."

Ibn Battuta was a 14th-century Moroccan traveler who, during his lifetime, covered nearly 73,000 miles—far surpassing Marco Polo's 7,500. What kind of passport, I wonder, did he carry?

"Travel leaves you speechless," Battuta wrote, "then turns you into a storyteller." How ironic that the most important object we carry on our journey is a book—filled only with the placeholders of our stories.

108 BELOVED OBJECTS

Silver Teapot
MOROCCO, 1994

During a Q &A at a travel writers' conference, I was asked which interview, in the course of my career, had been my favorite. It was a tough question. Over the years I've been privileged to interview many brilliant and strange people, from Buzz Aldrin to Grace Slick. But the interview that came to mind—the one that moved me most deeply—was my 1994 encounter with the Morocco-based writer and composer Paul Bowles.

My meeting with Bowles seemed fated. Striding up to the desk at the tourist bureau in Tangiers, I'd announced my desire to meet the author of The Sheltering Sky. The clerk regarded me with amusement; it was probably his 10th such request that week. Then a voice piped up behind me. A taxi driver wearing a white *djellaba* and red fez said he knew where Bowles lived. Honestly? "Honestly." Off we sped along the boulevards of Tangiers. He pulled up at a weathered apartment building, and told me the room number.

Sheepishly, I knocked on the door. The large male housekeeper who appeared was off-putting: Bowles was not to be disturbed. "I just want to convey my respect and gratitude," I replied. The man harrumphed. "Wait," he said, and closed the door. A moment later he reappeared: "Mr. Bowles will see you for five minutes."

I found Bowles sitting up in bed, a lit *kief* cigarette smoking in an ashtray amidst a riot of pill bottles upon his nightstand. He held out a papery hand. "I hope you didn't come to meet one of the last Beat writers," he warned me.

"You were never a Beat writer," I countered. "You were much more literary."

"Sit down," Bowles said, nodding toward the end of the bed.

His housekeeper brought in a small pot of tea.

We talked for hours, well into the evening—about writing, music, Morocco, travel, the future, old age, death… Bowles even questioned me about my habitual nail-biting: "It's surely not about hunger," he noted. When the sky grew dark, I regretfully took my leave. Bowles wrote down his address, and asked that I stay in touch.

"Thank you for your time—and for your friendship," I said.

"It was easy," he replied. To this day, I have never heard sweeter words.

Exiting the building a few moments later, I had to laugh: My taxi driver was waiting for me at the curb, the meter still running.

108 BELOVED OBJECTS

Pink Wooden Elephant
OAXACA, 1988

Guelaguetza means "to give a gift without expecting anything in return." Oaxaca's annual Guelaguetza festival is held on two consecutive Mondays in late July. Tribal groups from all over Mexico mass in the city's open stadium. They sing traditional songs, dance traditional dances, and throw gifts to the maniacal capacity crowd. Sometimes the objects are small: limes, tamales, packets of coffee or chilies. But just as often they are enormous, and potentially deadly: pineapples, papayas, and coconuts, catapulted into the stands.

The Guelaguetza took its present form in 1932. It descends from the Aztec *Lunes del Cerro*, during which a virgin was sacrificed to the goddess of corn. The dispensing of gifts to a crowd is almost as ancient. I read this in the fiesta's program:

> *"The lords and nobles gathered and gave food to men and women, large and small, for eight continuous days before the festival. At noon everyone received as many tamales as they could hold in one hand."*

How many tamales can a person hold in one hand? I think I could manage six, if I palmed three and then built a little pyramid—but given a few weeks of practice, who knows what might be possible?

In 1988 I was on assignment at Oaxaca's Guelaguetza, shooting pictures like mad. At one point I reached behind me into my photo bag, only to discover my zoom lens had been stolen.

Though I shrugged off the loss, Polo, my young local guide, was crestfallen—to the point where I thought he would cry. Oaxaqueños are honest people, he insisted, but pickpockets and other thieves come down from Mexico City to exploit the event and rob merrymakers.

When the festival ended, I led Polo into the craft market and, to show my unflagging love of Oaxaca, bought this pink *alibrije* elephant. The ears and tail come off, for easy transport. You may have it; I ask nothing in return.

108 BELOVED OBJECTS

Hewlett Packard OmniBook 300

OAKLAND, 1993

In November 1993, before I left my Oakland flat to circle the world without airplanes, I was gifted an OmniBook 300. The understanding was that I would use it to write short tales of my travels, which would then be sent by modem to California and featured on GNN: The Global Network Navigator, a pioneer of the World Wide Web.

The OmniBook 300 was the first ultra-light laptop. It weighed 2.9 pounds, had a full-size keyboard, a 9-inch monochrome screen, and a little mouse that popped out from the side. It came bundled with Microsoft Word and Excel. Incredible. Adorable. Indispensable. Most amazing, it could run all day on four AA batteries. See to left: There I am on March 6th, my 40th birthday, writing a blog from the Mars-like hell of the Mauritanian desert.

A few weeks later, at a café in central Turkey, a young mystic named Ishmael read the grounds at the bottom of my coffee cup. He predicted disaster: "You will lose your best friend," he warned. "Your confidant. The one you trust with your deepest secrets."

Sobering news, but my journey continued—through Syria and Saudi Arabia, from Dubai into Pakistan. By late May, I was on an overnight bus from India to Nepal. I slipped my daypack into the overhead rack, and dozed off. When we stopped for a toilet break in the middle of the night, my pack was gone: stolen. Inside was my OmniBook, with a month's worth of detailed, intensely personal writing. Ishmael's prediction had come true.

Dismayed, I paid for a week of ads in *The Kathmandu Post*, in Nepali, offering a large reward, no questions asked, for the laptop's return. No luck. At that point I visited a doctor friend in Kathmandu and asked him for Prozac. He shook his head. "This isn't chronic," he explained. "You have every reason to be depressed."

I bought a used laptop from a friend in Nepal, and did my best to rehash everything that had happened to me in Arabia, on the Gulf of Oman, and through Pakistan and India.

After I returned to the U.S., Hewlett Packard sent me a second OmniBook. I haven't used it since 1997. In my estimation, this ingenious relic belongs in an industrial design museum. Any place, really, besides the bottom of my closet.

108 BELOVED OBJECTS

Namlo (Tumpline)
NEPAL, 1979

In an article in the August 2017 issue of *The Atlantic*, Pippa Biddle gives a wonderful history of the tumpline, and explains why it's a better carrying strategy than backpacks: "When used properly," writes Biddle, "tumplines evenly channel weight down the strongest part of the body. They require good posture and don't allow for the sloppiness that can be hidden with a hip belt and shoulder straps. They also don't restrict lung expansion in the way that pack straps can, allowing for deeper and more even breathing, something that is especially important at high altitudes."

Even so, Westerners trekking in the Himalaya are reliably astonished by our first encounters with these *namlo* in action. Not only does it seem counterintuitive to carry a huge load with your head; the cargo itself is often surreal.

In the Autumn of 1979, I met a Nepali porter on the Annapurna trail. He was hoofing 120 bottles of soft drinks—a stack as tall as he was—from Pokhara to the mountain village of Tatopani: a three-day hike that gains (not counting steep ups and downs) nearly a mile in elevation.

A few days later, I thought I would be clever and try fixing my backpack to a tumpline. Bad idea. Within five minutes of carrying this moderate load—to the great amusement of the watching porters—I'd strained my neck. I don't think it's been the same since.

Nonetheless, I bought myself a namlo as a souvenir of Nepal—partly for its folksy macramé, but also as a cautionary reminder of my reckless naiveté.

108 BELOVED OBJECTS

Paper Money
KAZAKHSTAN, UZBEKISTAN, 1995

Though every airport has at least one gift shop, I always seem to leave foreign countries with a few stray notes and coins. Sometimes the terminals have a bin where travelers can donate their extra cash to a charity. The former Soviet republics did not. I thus imagined I'd give these bills away as souvenirs, or exchange them for drinks at one of those bars with foreign bills taped above the register. Neither happened.

It's hard to throw away money. It doesn't matter if it's from a country I'll never visit again, or if its value is lower than that of the real estate it takes up in my drawer. Nor does it matter if it's paper money or coins. Even a penny. Throwing money into a trash bin is just, well, disturbing. But the process of turning this money into something that could benefit another human being would require an insane investment of energy, time, and (of course) money.

My friend Rob Brezsny once stood on a street corner and tried to give money away to passersby. There were few takers; people were deeply suspicious. In 2011, at performances of monologist Mike Daisey's *The Last Cargo Cult*, ushers handed out legal tender to every person entering the theater—one bill per person, worth (depending on your luck) between one and 50 dollars. The sum total equaled the performer's projected earnings for the night. When the show ended, Daisey requested that people return the money to a large bowl in front of the stage. On some nights he received back much less than he distributed; on other nights, considerably more.

When I worked at San Francisco's Exploratorium in the 1970s, we had donation boxes set up by each exit. Admission was free, but the museum relied on contributions. At the end of each day, I asked a few of the "Explainers" (i.e., the teenage guides who wore red jackets and answered visitors' questions) to collect the donations in a big sack. I didn't learn until years later that many of the kids had stuffed the largest bills into their pockets. Maybe *that's* why I don't trust those airport donation bins.

These are the memories that come to my mind as I study this useless wad of currency. Can I throw it into the trash? Of course not. Can I donate it somewhere? Nope. Can I even *give* it away? That's up to you.

108 BELOVED OBJECTS

Heineken Havana 500th Anniversary Bottle
CUBA, 2019

The 16th of November, 2019, marked the 500th Anniversary of La Habana: the city of Havana. I planned to bring a group of 11 people to the celebration. Our preparations unfolded flawlessly, despite the scheming of an unhinged President (ours).

This was the fifth trip I'd organized to Cuba, and the only one during which we would spend a full week in the capital. It was also my first voyage abroad since my 2018 hospitalization, 20 months earlier. It wasn't going to be easy, that much I knew. My sciatica nerve is bedeviled by post-operative scars, my left leg throbs constantly, and I still can't reach up higher than my head. The journey would include some suffering. But it was an inquiry into what might be possible for me, going forward. I promised myself not to complain.

Among the participants were my old friend Steve, and his wife, Becca. I'd known them well when they lived in the Bay Area, back in the 1980s. After they moved to Portland I saw less of them, but our mutual affection endured. They were thrilled to join the trip.

Steve is in his 60s now. When he was 17 he was vagabonding, riding the rails across the U.S. Somewhere in Arizona, he jumped off a train car and missed. He ended up under the wheels. Steve lost both his legs: one above the knee, one below. With no medical help in sight, he pulled a length of rope from his backpack and tourniqueted his own horrific wounds. He held on somehow until an ambulance arrived, 20 minutes later.

Steve now walks on two high-tech prostheses, which he designed and built. He also uses a carved wooden cane. Though he hobbled some, he had as much energy as anyone in the group. One night at about 9, we were dropped off at Havana's Fabrica De Arte Cubano: a former factory, recently repurposed into a fabulous labyrinth of galleries, dance spaces, installations, theaters, and bars. By 11 p.m., nearly everyone had run out of steam and took the tour bus back to our hotel. Not Steve. He and I stayed until 1 a.m., threading our way through the crowded corridors, drinks in hand, enthralled by the dynamism of Cuba's contemporary art scene.

That was just one of the eight eye-opening nights we spent exploring Havana. And though I'm not sure how much Steve's influence had to do with it, I'll tell you one thing: I never complained.

108 BELOVED OBJECTS

Krishna Statue

INDIA, 1985

During my visit to India in 1985, Varanasi was a City of Liars: an opaque metaphor, like something out of Calvino's *Invisible Cities*. I was lied to about everything: my fare from the train station, the price of my lunch, the cost of a handkerchief.

As he rowed me onto the Ganges at dusk, my boatman announced that he would overturn our flimsy vessel—dumping me and my camera into the corpse-laden river—if I didn't double his already exorbitant fee. To underscore his threat, he pulled in the oars and began rocking the vessel violently from side to side.

I told him that I didn't have the money on me, that I never carried that much cash at one time. But my hotel was right by the riverside. He could come to my room to collect it if he returned me safely to shore.

Gamely he rowed me back. The instant the keel touched the muddy bank, I leaped from the boat and began running. He followed in pursuit, shouting, chasing me down the street with a stout oar ready in his hands.

I lost him in the Night Market, a maze of bulb-lit stalls packed with cotton sellers and goldsmiths, mangos and chess sets, woven silk brocades snapping open like iridescent fireworks. I rounded a bend and ducked into a shop selling small devotional statues. Here was something new: The shiny brass gods and goddesses came with accessories, like G.I. Joe. You could buy a crown for Ganesha, a skirt for Kali, a bow for noble Laxman.

This Krishna caught my eye: lover, prankster, and slayer of river demons. I paid a fair price for the figure, and almost as much for his flute—which, despite the merchant's assurance, is not really gold.

108 BELOVED OBJECTS

Frog Prince Bottle Opener
GUYANA, 2011

Searching for obscure creatures in an obscure country sums up the Guyana experience. The place is an environmental Eden that few people know about. Size-wise, it's a bit bigger than Washington state, but with only 15 percent of the population. It's also the only English-speaking country in South America. More than three-quarters of the land is still covered by virgin rainforest.

My guide, Wally Prince, was born in Guyana. He grew up watching TV, dividing his attention between wildlife documentaries and *The Cosby Show*. He's a gleeful expert on Guyana's flora and fauna, with an unnerving gift for detail.

"Watch out for pit vipers," he said as we circled a tree, on one of several sweltering hikes. "Those are mean guys. Imagine a rattlesnake eight feet long—with no rattle."

Guyana's jungles host many rare species: gorgeous birds like the cock-of-the-rock, the enormous *Victoria amazonica* water lily, stealthy jaguars, and colorful frogs. But the country's signature attraction is found at breathtaking Kaieteur Falls, which plunges into the Potaro River with a drop five times the height of Niagara.

After landing at a tiny airstrip near Kaieteur National Park, we began our short hike to the headwaters. I told Wally my personal obsession: to find Guyana's famous golden frog. I love frogs; they're fascinating creatures. In 2010, after watching Disney's *The Princess and the Frog*, I tried to snag "frogprince2010" as my Gmail address—alas, it was already taken.

Golden frogs are poison dart frogs, found only in this part of the Amazon. They like to hide inside giant tank bromeliads, perched near the pools of water that collect within the plant's broad green leaves. But golden frogs are notoriously skittish, and will leap away if disturbed.

With Kaieteur Falls roaring behind us, Wally crept from plant to plant, parting the broad green leaves to peer inside. Finally, with a wide-eyed grin, he gestured me over. Success. The jewel-like amphibian seemed lost in thought, serene in his (or her) chlorophyll cave. I set my camera to macro, and snapped several close-ups.

"Can you send me one of those?" Wally asked.

"Of course. What's your email address?"

"Got a pen? It's frogprince2010." he said. "At gmail.com"

Silk Purse with Frankincense

BLACK ROCK CITY, 2000 > 2019

There is a similarity between Israel, Cuba, and Burning Man: If you haven't been, you really can't weigh in on a debate about the place. But maybe that's true of anywhere.

    My first visit to Burning Man was in 2000. I was assigned to shoot video for The Adventure Zone, a short-lived online network. Few trips had terrified me more. I'm talking about nightmares and panic attacks, a week prior to my departure. The prospect of the desert heat, alkaline dust, naked mobs, and pounding EDM all added up to a perfect storm of "no thank you" for me. But I'd said yes. As usual.

Travel

I arrived ill-prepared, my Honda Civic packed with a pup tent, water, snacks, a beat-up bike, more water, and little else. After staking my tent into the hard strata of the ancient playa, I mounted my bike and rode off to get a feel for Black Rock City: the sudden metropolis that annually erupts, like Martian fungus, on the otherwise lifeless plain.

The grid of the City follows the pattern of a clock, and at the corner of 7:30 and Sex Drive I saw an inviting prospect: A serene-looking woman with flowing gray hair had set up a padded massage table, shaded by a pink canopy. I parked my bike, lay on my back, and allowed her to tune my chakras with a set of seven Tibetan singing bowls. Each vibrated with a pure, resonant frequency. The woman placed them in turn on my forehead, throat, solar plexus, and groin, and instructed me to breathe deeply.

This might have been a spell of utter relaxation, if not for the shrieks, screams, and moans coming from the adjoining camp—where a tattooed vixen in a fishnet bustier was shoving volunteer victims onto a rack, shackling their wrists and ankles with fur-lined handcuffs, and spanking them mercilessly with a ping pong paddle.

"I have to say," I told my masseuse, after the final bowl's vibration faded into silence, "that you ended up with a pretty noisy neighbor."

"Isn't it great?" she replied. "That's my daughter!"

Gifting is one of the "Ten Principles" created by Burning Man's co-founder, the late Larry Harvey, to define the ethos of the event—which is now celebrated worldwide. In August 2019, I returned from my 13th journey to Black Rock City. The gift I offered the burners with whom I forged a connection was the same one I'd given my sound masseuse in 2000: a silk pouch from Nepal, filled with crystals of Omani frankincense. As for me, the gift I've received has been profound: What I once dreaded so desperately is now a delight. So smell these crystals. Pack your tent. Bring plenty of water. Fear not.

Oil Lamp
ISRAEL, 2004

1.

I chose to celebrate my 50th birthday in Israel and Jordan, two places I'd never before visited.

Despite its awesome antiquity—or as a function of it—Israel was challenging, on many levels. There had been a bus bombing in Jerusalem the day before my arrival, and the country was on high alert. Israel, I quickly discovered, may be the only country on earth where you gladly stop your rented Hyundai to pick up a hitchhiker carrying an M16 assault rifle.

"It's not an M16," the teenage soldier corrected me. "It's an A3."
"What's that?"
"An M16 with an Israeli upgrade."

Nowhere in my travels had I encountered a dynamic more dysfunctional than the blood feud between the Israeli Jews and Palestinians. Another armed hitchhiker—this one a medic—told me of a plan to discourage suicide bombings by returning the bomber's remains wrapped in pork: "A sick solution," he admitted, "for a sick society."

It wasn't all bad. There was the Dead Sea, which cocooned my body in a scarf-like gossamer of salt; the tiny rolls of prayer pressed into the crevices of the Western Wall; the Marc Chagall windows of Abbell Synagogue at the Hadassah University Medical Center; exquisite raw honey on the kibbutz.

II.

But in full measure, it was all too much. So I departed Israel and celebrated my actual birthday in Jordan's astonishing Wadi Rum, exploring a familiar and beloved landscape: That desert was used as a location in *Lawrence of Arabia*, one of my two all-time favorite movies. So geeky am I that I'd actually brought along my Sony Walkman, loaded with the soundtrack from the film. Listening to Maurice Jarre's swelling Overture, as our Willys bounced between the sandstone arches and hoodoos, brought me to tears. Though I'm not religious, I recited what I find to be the most beautiful Jewish prayer; a prayer of gratitude, for having lived to reach this moment: sheheheyanu v'kiyimanu, v'higiyanu laz'man hazeh.

III.

The village of Beit Ummar sprawls over the grapevine and plum-covered hills just north of Hebron, in the West Bank. It resembles a hive of sandstone cubes, scattered across the undulations like weathered salt crystals. A group called The Christian Peacemakers Team had arranged my overnight visit. I was hosted by the family of Ghazi Brigieth—a 42-year-old Palestinian peacemaker who had created an interfaith organization with the self-explanatory name of Bereaved Families.

While Ghazi and I conversed, his 3-year-old son Yusef played in the yard. Ghazi told me a story about how, earlier, when Yusef thought he'd offended his father by saying a bad word, he pretended to take a gun out of his tunic and put the barrel in his mouth. "How clever he is!" Ghazi exclaimed drily. As the afternoon faded and the slow roll to dusk began, clever little Yusef picked up a black water bottle and put it to his mouth like a megaphone. "Mamnua a'tizjawol!" he cried out. "Mumnua a'tizjawol!" (Curfew! Curfew!)

IV.

Returning to Jerusalem, I faced a dilemma. What does one bring back as a keepsake from such an ambivalent journey? For myself, a beautiful silver kiddush cup, which I now use for the blessing over the holiday wine. And as an offering, this ancient oil lamp.

May there be light.

You can read the full set of dispatches from my Israel trip here: http://thingsasian.com/story/compromised-land-dispatches-israel-beyond

108 BELOVED OBJECTS

Meditating Buddha — Hello Kitty Mini-Towel

JAPAN, 2005

I'm fascinated by the way different Asian cultures treat images of the Buddha.

In Thailand, for example, sitting on the lap of a Buddha statue—a once-traditional photo-op for tourists visiting Siam's ancient capitals—is now strictly forbidden. Foreigners with Buddha tattoos risk being turned away at Immigration; even T-shirts with Buddha images are taboo. Actually damaging a Buddha can land you in a Thai prison, and smuggling drugs inside a hollowed-out Buddha statue—well, let's not even go there.

Nepal, where the historical Buddha was born, in 563 BC, takes a less draconian approach. Though Buddha images are respected, local businesses are happy to cash in on his panache: Buddha brand potato chips, Siddhartha Copy Center, early morning mountain flights aboard Buddha Air. And though the hand-lettered signs at Kathmandu's famous Monkey Temple warn *Don't Climb on Buddha!*, many Chinese tourists don't speak English.

Then, to confuse things altogether, there's Japan. In Kamakura, at the shrine of the Great Buddha, a street stall sells hard brown globs (attached to key chains), which are said to be boogers from the Enlightened One's nose. In nearby Nara, the Deer Park, the doors of the local police cars portray grinning Buddhas, shaking the hands of cartoon deer.

This small washcloth was made by Sanrio, the company that owns Hello Kitty—an icon as ubiquitous in Tokyo as plastic sushi. I love the way it integrates cats and buddhas: two of my favorite spiritual beings. It was intended to be given as a gift, but what, really, is it good for? Anything involving soil, or bodily fluids, seems sacrilegious. Unless, of course, it's used to polish Buddha statues—or serve as bedding for newborn kittens.

108 BELOVED OBJECTS

Two-Headed Shiva Drum (Damaru)

NEPAL, 1983

Teri and I met a begging *sadhu*, a Hindu holy man, on the streets of my neighborhood in Kathmandu. He wore long dreadlocks and heavy necklaces, and displayed on his forehead the vertical signs of a Shiva devotee. The mendicant carried a tall iron trident, another symbol of the Hindu pantheon's great Creator/Destroyer.

The sadhu's manner seemed friendly, and after a short chat we invited him to our hotel room at the Chhetrapati Guest House for tea and arrowroot biscuits.

The sadhu entered our cluttered room, looked around, and immediately pointed, with the focus of a bloodhound, at something in the corner. I followed his finger but saw nothing; just a small round table cluttered with a bunch of gear for our upcoming trek. Teri looked puzzled. I shook my head; there was nothing on the table we could spare.

"That! That!" He wagged his finger up and down, almost shouting.

Teri lit up. "He wants a flower!" she exclaimed brightly. Indeed, there was a small brass vase of flowers on the table. Teri plucked one out and brought it to the sadhu, smiling. He threw it to the floor. "No! *There!*"

Aha. There was a bottle of Johnnie Walker on the table. The sadhu wanted whiskey.

"No," I said. "No whiskey."

He stormed angrily out of the room. Teri and I looked at each other. We shrugged; then we laughed. I got up to use the shared bathroom, just down the hall.

The sadhu was standing on the closed toilet lid, urinating all over the walls and floor. I shouted with rage and found the manager, who dragged the sadhu outside and—furious with me for welcoming the sadhu in the first place—hosed down the fouled bathroom.

When I next saw the sadhu, he greeted me with a wave. He may have been satisfied, all things considered, to have taught me a lesson: When in Asia, play by Asia's rules. If you plan to hang out with an acolyte of Shiva, the ultimate stoner, Lipton's won't cut it.

108 BELOVED OBJECTS

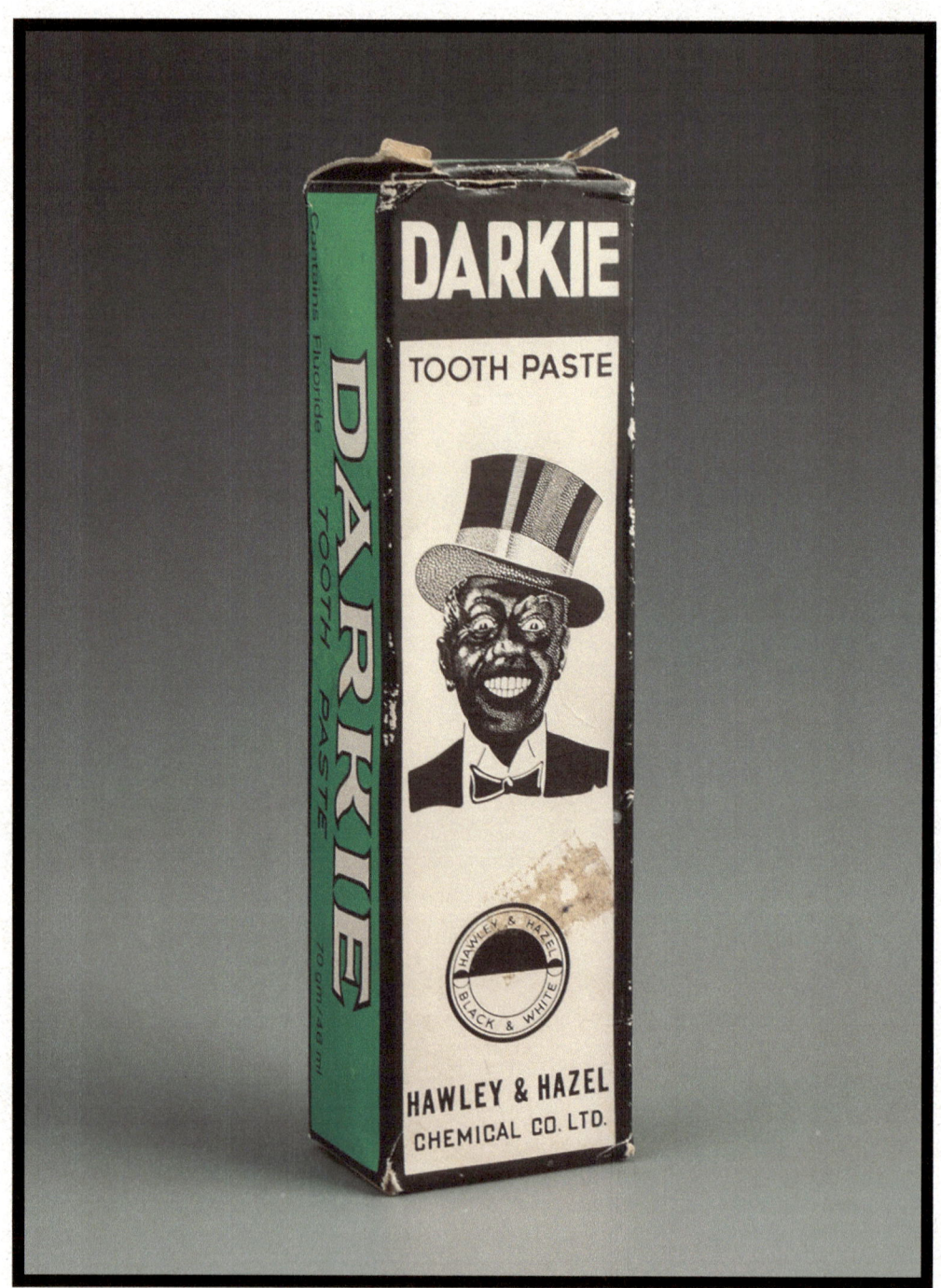

Darkie Toothpaste
THAILAND, 1979

I know. I couldn't believe it either.

But Thais, at least in 1979, were not always 100-percent aware of what various English words and phrases meant. One afternoon, I saw a prepubescent girl walking sweetly down the street, holding her mother's hand. The girl's T-shirt showed two halves of a grapefruit, one over each breast. The message below said, "Squeeze My Juicy Grapefruits!" As for myself, I was peeved and baffled as every single school-age Thai boy on the street ran up to me and demanded to know, "*Where are you going!?*" It took me many years to figure out that they'd simply fumbled an idiom. What they actually meant was, "*How is it going?*"

Darkie toothpaste, made in China by a company called Hawley and Hazel, was introduced in 1933. The image was a parody of Al Jolson. When Colgate-Palmolive acquired the brand in 1985, they changed its name to "Darlie" (really?) and promised the product's sales would be confined to Asia. The image was also changed, and now displays a top-hatted dandy of ambiguous racial pedigree.

Fifteen years later, I saw something that gave me an equivalent shock. This was in a general store in Riyadh. The shop sold toasters and irons and blenders and, as is often the case, the packaging displayed images of smiling women using the appliances. Such immodesty is not kosher in Saudi Arabia, and some pious worker had been tasked with taking a black marker and blotting out the legs, bare arms, and faces of the comely models—leaving only their eyes.

It was a decidedly blackface look. In this case, though, no racial slur was intended. The motive was institutionalized misogyny.

108 BELOVED OBJECTS

Snow Globe
NEW ORLEANS, 2019

Dwayne and I embarked on a road trip to the Deep South, as we call it up north. We began in Montgomery, Alabama. Our first destinations were the two projects created by civil rights activist and attorney Bryan Stevenson: The Legacy Museum (i.e., the slavery museum) and The National Memorial for Peace and Justice (i.e., the lynching memorial). I had wanted to see these places with my closest African American friend, and didn't feel sheepish asking Dwayne to make the trip with me.

The slavery museum narrates the bleakest poles of the Black American experience: from slavery to mass incarceration. To visit that place, and descend afterwards into the solemn pit of the lynching memorial, is to understand that racism in America is an open wound.

After Montgomery we drove north to Selma, parked in the town, and walked together across the Edmund Pettus Bridge. From there we steered west into Mississippi, en route to New Orleans. We avoided the interstate. Our hope was to see the "real" Mississippi. I guess we didn't get deep enough; through our windows it was all strip malls and churches, Walmarts and frozen yogurt shops. The one exception was the tiny town of Lumberton, population 2,228. An intersection split its business district: a Family Dollar, gas station, and small grocery store.

We passed through Lumberton, Dwayne at the wheel. A minute later he drew in his breath. "Aw, shit," he said. I glanced in the side view mirror, dismayed to see flashing blue lights.

The cop ambled over from his patrol car. A little pudgy, vivid blue eyes, right out of central casting. His uniform button-down was open, over a yellow Lumberton PD T-shirt. "Good afternoon, gentlemen," he said. "Do you know why I pulled you over?"

Of course Dwayne knew why he'd been pulled over. And it wasn't the rented Ford with the out-of-state plates. "No, sir, I really don't."

"Well," said the officer, "you ran that stop sign back there at the intersection."
"Officer..." Dwayne shook his head. "I stopped for that stop sign."
"No, sir," the cop replied. "I watched you blow right past it."
"I was watching," I offered, absurdly. "He really did stop."
The policeman ignored me. "License and registration, please."

Dwayne had his wallet ready, and handed it through the window. The officer flipped it open, studied it for a few seconds, and held it back to Dwayne.

"Thank you for your service," he intoned respectfully. "Y'all have a good day." And he walked away.

Lt. Dwayne Newton had retired from the San Francisco Fire Department three years earlier, but he got to keep his badge. Nonetheless, he seemed as astonished as I was. "That could have gone a number of ways," he reflected. Then his eyes lit up. He leaned back out his open window. "Hey!," he called. The officer turned around.

"I'll make you a deal," Dwayne said.
Utter befuddlement on the cop's side. "Excuse me? I'm letting you guys go."
"No, no, no," Dwayne said. "Listen: If you send me a Lumberton PD T-shirt, I'll send you an SF Fire Department T-shirt."

"Sure!" They laughed together, and exchanged business cards.

No place—not even my friendship with Dwayne—is color-blind. But when we get a glimpse of what that world might look like, it stays with us. Still, we made full stops clear through to Louisiana.

108 BELOVED OBJECTS

Plastic Dove with Koranic Verses
IRAN, 1999

It's difficult to find souvenirs in Iran; one searches for that irresistible blend of beauty, authenticity, and kitsch. But as any visitor to an Islamic country soon learns, the most captivating expression of any Muslim culture is its calligraphy. This plastic dove bears on its wings verses from the Quran, along with a single Arabic expression on its chest: *Masha'Allah*. What wonders God has willed!

I hoped for an opportunity to utter this phrase in the thousand-year-old Iranian city of Isfahan, where—as the only American tourist in vast Imam Khomeini Square—I awaited a total eclipse of the sun.

It was a beautiful afternoon, warm and clear, and the square soon filled up with thousands of Iranian families. As the invisible moon began to move across the face of the sun, the crowd gradually became silent. All eyes were on the thinning solar crescent—until, shockingly, a group of bearded youths sitting near me unzipped a carpet bag, pulled out automatic weapons, and began firing into the air. Pumping their fists and shouting angry slogans, they set an American flag ablaze. Television crews from all over the Middle East, assembled in the square for the eclipse, rushed over to film the outburst.

At that moment, something extraordinary happened. Every man, woman, and child sitting close to me rose spontaneously to their feet and, without speaking a word, formed a tight ring around me. A little boy held my wrist; an elderly man placed his hand on my shoulder. Several women, cloaked in *rusari*, stood stalwart by my side. This circle of strangers shielded me until the pop-up protest ended—at which point the radical Islamists calmly stashed their weapons, and sat down to enjoy the eclipse with the rest of us.

As the sun finally disappeared behind by the moon, its fiery corona blazed against the stars. A spontaneous cry rose from the crowd. *Masha'Allah! Masha'Allah!* I joined right in. It no longer mattered that I'd found no key rings in Persepolis, or snow globes at the Tomb of Hafez. My souvenir from Persia is this story.

108 BELOVED OBJECTS

Travel

Marble Ganesha

NAGDA, INDIA, 2007

I took my mom to India for her 75th birthday. Okay, maybe India wasn't her first choice. But when I present people with options, so I'm told—be they restaurants, films, hiking trails—I usually manipulate things so that we end up where *I* want to go.

My mom, Roslyn, is a conservative Jewish woman. She was bat mitvah'd at age 66. She keeps a kosher home, and I had many apprehensions about how she—*we*—would fare, traveling together for the first time since I was about 10.

In fact, she was a fabulous companion. During our two-week journey through South Asia, I came to realize that it was she—and not, as I'd long believed, my restless, highly distracted father—who had bequeathed me the essential tools of a traveler. Open-minded, interested in everyone, delighted with *palak paneer* and potato samosas, Mom made a wonderful impression everywhere we went, and surprised me continually.

One such surprise occurred during our visit to the Saas Bahu Temple complex, near Udaipur. The 1,000-year-old temples are covered with exquisite carvings (though many were defaced by Moghul invaders). A craftsman had set up a table by the entrance, and was selling small, abstract statues of Ganesha: the God of Auspicious Beginnings, Protector of Writers and Travelers, Remover of Obstacles.

I ducked into one of the temples, and when I emerged my mother was bargaining with the vendor. I was astonished. Idolatry is strictly forbidden in Judaism. Though I'd succumbed years ago to the "Golden Calf syndrome" (i.e., the seduction of many Jews, as they wander through Asia, by local gods and goddesses), I never dreamed that my mom, who lights the Sabbath candles every Friday, would fall victim.

"Mom!" I exclaimed. "You're actually buying yourself a Hindu deity!"

"It may be a deity to you," she replied serenely, accepting the wrapped elephant-god, "but it's a souvenir to me."

108 BELOVED OBJECTS

Dolphin Tooth Necklace
SOLOMON ISLANDS, 1987

There were no tour buses in the Solomon Islands, no local Wonders of the World, no towering temples or Monkey Dances at the ends of well-paved roads. Roads themselves, in fact, were scarce. It quickly became obvious that I would need to find my own way.

The South Pacific nation is composed of 1,000 islands. Nearly 100 dialects have evolved across the archipelago, each spoken by a small, localized population. A powerful loyalty exists among people who share the same language; this is called the *wantok* (Pijin for "one talk") system. Wantoks are tribal kin; one wantok will always help another out.

I knew that a writer—of any nationality—would qualify as one of my wantoks. In the capital of Honiara, I met and befriended a local author named Julian Maka'a. He had just published a short story collection (*The Confession and Other Stories*), and his dream was to return to his family's village on the island of Makira and record the traditional tales of his clan. His uncle Moses was a healer; his great-grandfather, a sort of mayor. Julian's mother, fondly known as "Sau," was one of Makira's revered mystics. "She 'dream dances'," Julian told me, "and awakens to teach these dances—and their enchanted songs—to the village women." During the previous 10 years, Sau had brought more than 25 such dances from the dream-world to Makira.

There would be a ritual feast in the village in three weeks; preparations were already underway. With Julian's blessing—and his uncle's phone number—I took the inter-island flight to Makira, and was welcomed as a guest in the tiny village.

One night, Sau and the women of her village assembled to perform the dream dances for me. Eighteen women swayed beneath the stars, clapping and shouting in synchronous rhythm as Sau and three village elders chanted the mesmerizing songs. The dances were simple, but full of pantomime and innuendo that I could not understand.

I was rapt for the first hour, attentive for most of the second, drifting off by the third. But the dances went on and on. The women began to giggle, and lose their timing. Even the irrepressible Sau began to sound hoarse. Finally, Julian's uncle understood the problem. He leaned over to me and whispered that—according to local custom—it was up to the guest of honor to say when the dances should end.

They ended very shortly after that. I left the following morning, this lovely but somewhat disturbing necklace my parting gift from the remarkable Sau.

108 BELOVED OBJECTS

Vajra
LHASA, TIBET, 1994

There are a few beloved objects I cannot give away. But the rules of this project require that everything appearing here be gifted. So this copper *vajra*, or "thunderbolt"—a Tibetan symbol of the diamond-like clarity of the awakened mind—must stand in for the most valuable object I own.

In May of 1994, during my around-the-world overland odyssey, I traveled by car from Kathmandu to Lhasa. Though I'm not an avid shopper, there was something I wanted to find in Tibet. I was seeking a ring in the shape of a vajra. But also: It had to be *thogchag*.

The word *thogchag* means "sky iron." Tibetans believe that, eons ago, a war erupted between the gods and demigods. In the thick of battle, many small objects fell to Earth. Appearing as amulets, rings, buckles, and talismans, these ancient objects were forged in heaven, created from lost alloys of iron, bronze, copper—even material from meteorites.

Visiting an open-air market in Lhasa, I bought a sack of tangerines from a young man with ruddy, sun-scarred cheeks. The crimson braid woven into his black hair placed him from Kham, in eastern Tibet. Around his neck, on a thin red cord, he wore a simple ring, iridescent in the sunlight. When I expressed my admiration, he let me try it on. The well-burnished thogchag ring—in the shape of a vajra—fit my finger perfectly.

"How much you give?", the young K asked me. "No, no, no," I replied, horrified. "I can't buy this from you." I'd seen enough fake thogchag to know this was the real thing. It was an heirloom, many centuries old. "*How much?*" he insisted.

If I didn't buy the ring, another traveler would.

The ring has been on my finger for more than 25 years. I often wonder about the previous owners—all likely Tibetans, their lives a vast unknown to me. And I marvel, of course, at the vagaries of fate that delivered the ring to my hand. Even today, the object awes me. It's like something from a Marvel comic (Thor's hammer, or Dr. Strange's Eye of Agamotto), waiting to bequeath me its secret power.

Someday, I may find out what that power is. But I suspect a similar magic lies dormant in every vajra—even the one here—as it awaits its destined caretaker.

Gifts

I'd never been more terrified in my life. It was May, 1970. I was 16 years old, sitting on the train from Hicksville to Manhattan. Months earlier, I had written a five-page fan letter to my favorite author, who happened to live in Sri Lanka. Out of nowhere came a postcard telling me he was in New York, and inviting me to pay him a visit.

He was staying at the Chelsea Hotel. I'd put on my only sports jacket and boarded the Long Island Railroad in the 90-degree heat. The train was late, of course. When we pulled into Penn Station, I jumped off and sprinted toward 23rd Street. By the time I got to the Chelsea I was slick with sweat, the manila envelope holding two of my science-fiction stories limp under my arm.

Arthur C. Clarke greeted me at his door, grinning widely and shaking my hand. A portable typewriter sat on a table by the window, a breeze crackling the sheet of paper nested beneath the roller. He offered me tea; I loosened my tie.

We talked about his life as a writer, his work with Stanley Kubrick on *2001: A Space Odyssey*, and the ongoing Apollo program. The U.S. was landing men on the moon every few months, and Clarke co-hosted the live coverage on TV with his friend Walter Cronkite. I did a lot of nodding.

It took nearly an hour to work up my courage. "I wonder," I said, stammering, "if you'd read these stories I brought. I think they're pretty good." Clarke's face flashed, so briefly, with horror. Years later I'd understand: that sinking feeling of being cornered, and asked to look at an unproven writer's work. But I'd never come up with an alibi as good as his.

"I just can't do it," he said, shaking his head, leaning forward over his knees. "My publisher forbids it. Because there's a chance that—even unconsciously—I might steal one of your ideas."

Made perfect sense to me.

And then it was time to go. I slipped my sports coat on over my white shirt, and asked to use the bathroom. In a flash it was over—the greatest moment of my young life.

Until I left the Chelsea Hotel. There, in the kiln of the New York spring, I remembered: I'd left the manila envelope, with my stories, on Clarke's bathroom sink.

Shame exploded over me like a tsunami. I could not possibly go back to Clarke's room to reclaim it. He may have already gone into the bathroom himself, seen the packet, and cursed the manipulative moocher who had left it there. That quickly, the entire tenor of our encounter turned inside-out, like a sudden switch of the Earth's magnetic poles. My North Star had dropped south.

I took the train home. There was no way to even speak of the incident, so I hid my unforgiveable blunder behind a bright narrative. And tried to push the whole thing out of my head.

A few weeks later, my mother knocked on my bedroom door. I recognized the envelope she held out to me, my name in loose cursive, the return address the scene of my crime.

Inside were my stories. Clarke had gone over each one with a red Flair pen, highlighting my most grievous errors. There were many. One example that stays with me was a paragraph where I had my space explorers bouncing around on Saturn. "A little difficult," Clarke inscribed, "as Saturn is a gas giant!"

I read through his edits with a sinking heart. But then, at the end of the second story, he'd switched colors. "Did you leave these here by 'accident?'," he'd written in green. "In any case, I'd say you still have about a million words of writing to do—but you're just about where I was at sixteen."

This was his second lie. But it was also the greatest gift I've ever received.

108 BELOVED OBJECTS

Incense Burner

KATHMANDU, NEPAL, 1979

My family moved from Arlington, Massachusetts, to Plainview, Long Island, in 1963.

There was almost nothing I liked and very little I remember about growing up on Long Island. On special weekends, though, my parents would make a trip to the huge enclosed flea market at Roosevelt Field—built near the airport from which Charles Lindberg had begun his nonstop transatlantic flight in 1927.

The vendors at Roosevelt Field sold mainly clothes and purses and costume jewelry, packaged foods and knickknacks. It was a great place for a kid to wander around. My default destination was a stall selling imports from India. Amid the kitsch was a display of incense burners, and boxes of cone incense: sandalwood, pine, rose. For some reason, these obsessed me. The exotic scents were like trading cards—even on my limited allowance I wanted to collect the complete set.

Another memorable institution on Long Island was the Westbury Music Fair. The theater had a circular stage, somewhat below the surrounding seats. In April 1968 I saw The Doors perform there; tickets were $5. A few months later, Ravi Shankar played. During his concert, an incense burner sat on the stage, and a trippy aroma permeated the room. After the concert ended, and the musicians had left, I hurried down to see if there were any partially burned incense sticks I might take home. Indeed there were. As I was gathering my loot, I felt a hand on my shoulder. "What are you doing, young man?"

It was Ravi Shankar. Stammering, I explained myself. "Wait here," he instructed. He walked off, and returned a few moments later with a long, foil-wrapped package. "These were made especially for me, in Bangalore," he said. "Please enjoy them on special occasions."

Inside were three long, fragrant sticks of Ravi Shankar's personal incense. I lit the final one 11 years later, age 25, after safely returning from my first journey to Nepal and India.

108 BELOVED OBJECTS

Painted Cardboard Bird
SANTA CRUZ, 1977

After graduating from UC Santa Cruz in 1977, I moved onto a 42-foot lobster boat in the yacht harbor. My goal was to write a book, but the main character was a sculptor—and I knew very little about modern art. During my research I discovered (and became enthralled with) the playful mobiles, "stabiles," and wire sculptures of Alexander Calder. His use of color, sense of humor, and utter lack of pretension, all were qualities my protagonist ought to possess.

But to truly understand an artist's life, I'd have to become an artist myself—and this would require more space than a boat cabin.

A row of red clapboard houses stood precariously on a bluff above Front Street. Answering an ad for a housemate, I knocked at one of the doors.

The four-bedroom bungalow was occupied by a lesbian couple. The month-to-month lease was held by Bonnie LaQuatara—a cautious, narrow-faced, but warm-eyed former addict whose newly taken last name reflected her love of New Orleans' French Quarter. Bonnie and her partner interviewed me, then nodded at each other.

"You can move in," she said, "on one condition: Don't bother me with bullshit. Don't tell me I drank your milk, or left dishes in the sink. But if you decide to go to the beach at 3 a.m. to build sand castles, feel free to pound on my door."

My rent would be $75 a month for two rooms, one of which I could convert—as had Bonnie—into a studio. As a moving-in gift, Bonnie painted me this bird. It hung above my workbench, where I made art for more than a year. It was so much fun, such a total joy, that I abandoned my book idea completely and concentrated fully on creating sculptures.

We never did build sand castles together. Bonnie moved back to New Orleans. I visited her there in 1979, on my eventual way to Greece. She'd landed in a drab, cockroach-infested flat near Dauphine Street, and was drinking again. I drank with her for a few days, then left for New York.

Is she still alive? I wonder. I'd like to tell her that she changed my life. And that this bird still transports me, back through time and space, to that fearless, fecund year we shared in our now-demolished bungalow.

108 BELOVED OBJECTS

Glass Bead Necklaces
NEPAL (1979 THROUGH 2018)

Near the Indrachowk temple, I ducked into a narrow lane and found myself in a labyrinth of cubicles, surrounded by a million strands of glass beads in a thousand shimmering colors. They dangled in bunches from hooks and hangers, like the seed pods of hallucinatory plants. Each string held hundreds of the tiny beads... These strands may be combined in infinite combinations, like jelly beans. Muslim merchants in white skullcaps sat in stalls no bigger than phone booths, cross-legged on white cushions, bare light bulbs suspended above their heads...

- abridged from Snake Lake

A recurring question during my visits to Kathmandu is: What to bring back for my lady friends? In love with everything (and everyone), I always buy too much—almost everything that catches my eye. As a result, I'm in possession of bins filled with unclaimed statues, textiles, *thangkas* (devotional Buddhist paintings), and jewelry. While these baubles seemed irresistible when I bought them, none have found their fated owners.

Over the years, much of the magic has vanished from urban Kathmandu, hidden by clouds of dust, smog, smoke. But the Indrachowk bead market—perhaps because of its segregation from mainstream city life, both physically and racially—is an exception. Watching the Muslim merchants bind the hallucinatory strands together, using golden thread and a whirling, hand-held bob, is a hypnotic demonstration of skill so practiced it seems like sleight-of-hand. Time after time, I'm tricked into believing that the magic I witness in that market will translate to the gift itself. It never does. The necklaces, once home, never look as exotic as they did under those incandescent bulbs.

Still, every trip I've made to Nepal—from 1979 to 2018—has included a trip to the bead market. A friend in Alaska once told me that his ex-girlfriend's garage was "filled with broken chainsaws." Mine overflows with unclaimed necklaces. They really are pretty. And I think they were in fashion, once. Maybe they've come back.

Take these, please. There are plenty more where they came from.

108 BELOVED OBJECTS

Juju Protection Belt
SENEGAL, 1994

As Sally and I prepared to leave Senegal, Malang disappeared into his tiny bedroom. He opened a weathered chest of drawers, and returned with two narrow leather belts. Each was inlaid with small white cowrie shells.

"These *ju-ju* belts are for removing obstacles that may lie in your path." Malang dangled them in front of us like dead garden snakes. "You wear them beneath your clothing." He demonstrated on me, fastening the belt around my waist. There were two eyelets. "These will allow you to pass effortlessly across borders, and will be especially useful in places where people would harass or injure you. Close one loop for slight danger, both loops if the danger is extreme."

Malang had been our guide since we'd arrived in Dakar. He and I had the same birthday, March 6th, though he was a few years younger. He had driven us all around rural Dakar, introducing us to the most powerful local *marabouts* and shamans, male and female. Though assumedly Muslim, some specialized in the making and blessing of protective or wish-fulfilling ju-jus. These talismans came in infinite varieties, cobbled together from an unnerving assortment of animal parts: goat skins, beaver pelts, iguana hides and crocodile leather; buzzard claws, monkeys' paws, goat teeth, rat skulls, porcupine quills, cat whiskers, rams' horns, tortoise shells, hawk wings… In comparison, Malang's offerings to us were yawningly tame.

Our plan was to depart Dakar, travel up the coast to St. Louis (the Senegalese version), enter Mauritania, and traverse the bitterly contested sands of Western Sahara north to Morocco.

Mauritania was bleak and unwelcoming. We had the added misfortune of entering the country during the hypoglycemic holiday of Ramadan. The entire population was fasting, the more devout going so far as to spit out their own saliva before swallowing. Still, our ju-jus lay coiled in our backpacks.

But the desert crossing, through Western Sahara to Morocco, was a harrowing adventure. Granted passage on a British expedition bus, we set off along a sand-covered road seeded with hidden landmines. A previous bus, owned by the same outfitter, had been badly damaged by one such mine (no one, fortunately, was killed). And our only guide across this potentially lethal landscape was a crude map, drawn on a paper napkin by a bribed border officer.

"Buckle up," advised Sally, pulling Malang's ju-ju belt from her backpack. "Both loops."

And here I am to tell the tale.

108 BELOVED OBJECTS

Gifts

Maggie Award
FOR STORY IN VIRTUOSO LIFE MAGAZINE, 2004

"I cannot abide by the judgment of other people, because if you accept it when they say you deserve an award, then you have to accept it when they say you don't."

- Woody Allen

Is it true, what Woody says? I honestly don't know. My closet is filled with awards like this one, but I still couldn't get *The New York Times* to review my best book. Any of my books, actually.

I'd like to believe that all my silver statuettes and Lucite trophies and Lowell Thomas Travel Journalism Awards point to some meaningful achievement. But sometimes they seem hollow: cut-rate reminders of how greedily I've dined on low-hanging fruit.

Will someone please sit on my laurels for me?

108 BELOVED OBJECTS

Painted Plate from Cuba
MILL VALLEY, 2005

"What I've come to realize is that I can't do anything to make you happy," Tig said. "But you can easily make me unhappy."

She said more, of course, backing it all up with specific examples from various occasions, public and private. All were accurate. In every case, I completely got what a schmuck I'd been. I know now that my conduct welled up from a deep reservoir of dissatisfaction with life itself—a longing for unattainable perfection so pervasive that I viewed every instance, every moment, in a negative light.

Maybe part of what "cured" me—although it's questionable that I'm cured—was Cuba. When I first visited the island in 2011, I was at a point in my life where nothing, not even travel, seemed fresh. But Cuba is a place where people live under a constant cloud of imperfection, looking instead at the silver lining. They had much to teach me.

During that first visit I spoke with a man named Armando, 73, who had fought at *Playa Giron*: the Bay of Pigs. He summarized his country's bittersweet brand of socialism with a quote from Cuban poet José Martí: "The sun has spots," wrote Martí. "The ungrateful only speak of the spots. The grateful talk about the light." Armando's words took a while to sink in. But once they did—especially after my illness—I shifted my focus to gratitude.

This hand-painted plate was a gift from Tig after her own trip to Cuba. It's beautiful and sexy, and I love it. But a friend dropped by the other day and, exasperated by my clutter, curated the art jammed onto my fireplace mantel. I had to admit: It looked so much better without the clutter of so many indispensible objects. So I'm letting go of this plate—but I'll never forget Cuba's embrace.

108 BELOVED OBJECTS

Gifts

Autographed Ping Pong Ball
SRI LANKA, 1997

When my brother Jordan and I were kids, our dad set up a ping pong table in our downstairs recreation room. It barely fit, and we'd often collide with the walls behind us as we hustled to return each other's serves, slams, and slices. We played for hours every day. I took one rubber-nubbed paddle and spray painted it gold. This newly minted "Golden Paddle" went to the victor of our matches: a bitterly contested trophy.

I play some ping pong as an adult, though not as well. Still, I never turn down a game.

During each of my three visits to Sri Lanka—in 1984 and 1997 on writing assignments, and in 2005 as a member of a tsunami relief team—my friend Arthur Clarke invited me to the Otter Club, a recreational compound not far from his home in Colombo. I'd first met the author and futurist when I was 16, after he responded to a fan letter I'd written him. We remained friends until his death in 2008. Clarke had a fierce passion for ping pong. We played at the Otter Club's indoor tables, out of the brutal equatorial sun.

He beat me consistently during my first visit, and throughout my second, even though he was steadying himself with a cane. He was an infuriating opponent, gloating gleefully throughout each game and chortling over every victory.

Clarke had suffered from polio as a child, and in his later years developed post-polio syndrome. When I visited Sri Lanka in 2005, after the Indian Ocean tsunami, he was in and out of a wheelchair. But he challenged me again, rising unsteadily and gripping the edge of the ping pong table with his free hand as he played.

I managed to win that match.

I'm not proud of what I did next: I asked Clarke to sign the balls we'd used, as material proof that I'd finally beaten him. A dubious prize, compared to the Golden Paddle.

108 BELOVED OBJECTS

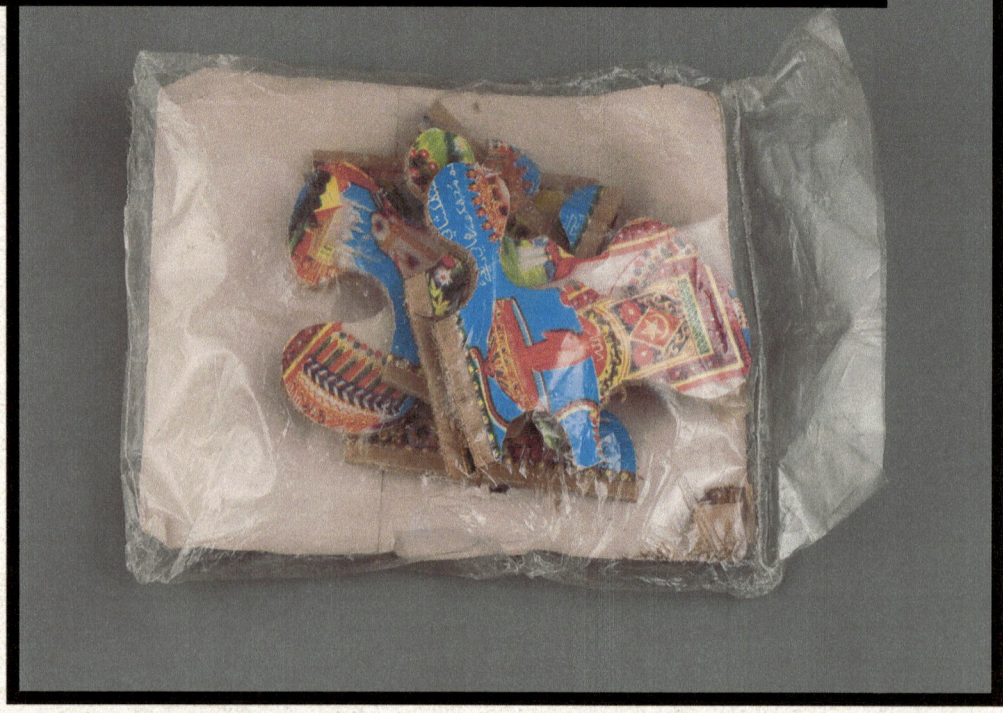

Puzzle Horse
INDIA, 1983

Walking through the Ajanta Cave temples in Aurangabad, India, I had a revelation. In one of the ancient wall murals—still vivid and clear, despite being at least 1,500 years old—I saw a scene I recognized. It wasn't that I remembered it from a guidebook, folktale, or art lecture. I remembered *being there*: actually being one of the characters in the scene. I saw myself in the mural, painted by an unknown hand in the distant past.

At that instant a storm of memories, complete with impossibly vivid details, flooded my mind. I recalled the names of the people around me that long-ago day; the reason for our gathering; my role in the scene; even the temperature of the air that cool afternoon, many centuries ago.

During the next several years I set to work writing about my life and experiences during that long-lost lifetime. I felt I had been touched by a force larger than myself. Honoring those memories was a calling: the most important project ever bequeathed to me.

I worked on the book first in Kathmandu, then in Santa Cruz, and continued wrestling with it when I moved to the Bay Area. The first few chapters came effortlessly. But the most intriguing part of the story—what became of "me" (or whatever you want to call that spark of consciousness) between the distant past and now—was a complete mystery. I had no memories at all of the in-between centuries; only of that life, and this one. There was a vast gap, and no bridge across it. My story needed that binding agent.

My single visit to the Ajanta Caves occurred when I was 29. Since then I've published scores of stories, and seven books. A few of them please me very much. But none of them is the one I once felt destined, even chosen, to write.

Over the years, I've come to accept that I may never write that book. Letting go of that inspiration haunts me. Yet try as I might, I can't seem to find my way through the labyrinth. It's as if I'd been solving a marvelous puzzle, only to discover that the most critical piece—the ones that would make it all fit together—are missing.

I don't blame myself. But sometimes I do feel I was given a profound gift, and wasn't smart enough, or persistent enough, to unwrap it.

108 BELOVED OBJECTS

Ceramic Bud Vase

BHUTAN, 2002

When I was a teen, still in junior high, my family went out one night to a fancy Chinese restaurant on Long Island. The china itself was beautiful, every piece decorated with the same floral motif. My eye was drawn to the little sugar bowl. I announced that I liked it, in a cagey way.

My parents suspected my intentions. I'd done some petty shoplifting around that time. I'm not proud of it. I'd even been caught, once, and brought home by the police! So now my mother's eyes were on me. And there were Chinese waiters everywhere. There was no way to do the misdeed without being seen.

When we left, it was dark out. We walked toward our car, a green Dodge Coronet. "Did you take the bowl?" my father asked me directly.

"No," I replied, but showed him a ceramic soup spoon. My brother, silently, revealed a saucer.

My father had grown up in a rough neighborhood, and possessed some skills we lacked. He shook his head, and took the sugar bowl out of his coat.

This was an isolated incident. Ours was not a family of thieves; far from it. My parents were usually obsessively honest, and after my punkish teen phase I followed that line. Even in 2000, on assignment for *Yoga Journal* in Bhutan, I had very mixed feelings about taking this small but elegant bud vase from my room in Thimpu's Hotel Riverside.

I like to think that I spoke with the management first, and that they offered it to me as a gift. Maybe that's what happened. Yes, I'm sure it was.

108 BELOVED OBJECTS

Martini Glasses
BERKELEY, CA, 2003

This is a set of racing car martini glasses (how cool is that?) created for me by Berkeley artist Stephanie Lesh.

I met Stephanie and her then-lover Les while trekking in Nepal's Annapurna range. It was November, and we were staying in a rustic tea house in the village of Hinko, sleeping on wooden platforms and eating *chapatis* with peanut butter and jam. That was more or less the standard of comfort on Nepal's treks in 1983.

The day after meeting around the open cooking hearth, four of us—Stef, Les, me, and my girlfriend Teri—took a day hike to the Annapurna Sanctuary. The magnificent granite walls and razor white peaks of the world's tenth-highest mountain soon rose around us. We spied a small, sheltered cave along the trail, and had an inspiration: Why not return to Hinko, retrieve our gear, and spend the night in the glorious Sanctuary itself? We embraced in gleeful agreement.

There was one problem with our plan: By the time we got back to that approximate spot, the sun was setting. We quickly lost the trail. Cold, stoned, and somewhat desperate, we decamped on the rocky ground and ate our only provisions: cold chapatis and M&M'S. Though it was still early evening, the temperature plummeted. We had no choice but to crawl into our down mummy bags, eat the Valium in my first aid kid, and try to sleep through the frigid Himalayan night, 13,000 feet above the distant sea.

That was how I spent Thanksgiving evening, 1983.

Les and Teri are pretty much out of the picture, but Stephanie and I remain friends. Her daughter Celia, now in her early 30s, is my goddaughter.

Stefla (as I call her) is a wonderful artist, and these glasses are cute, but I've switched to straight bourbon. And, as you know, I'm getting rid of things I love. But we'll always have Hinko.

108 BELOVED OBJECTS

Communications Satellite Tree Ornament
DATE UNKNOWN

There are objects in my life with sketchy origins. This silvery satellite[1] was possibly a gift from David McCutchen—an artist and inventor who appears in several of these stories. We met in 1980, when I was an editor at the *Santa Barbara News & Review*. He, like me, is a fan of spaceships, robots, and dinosaurs.

Though I don't celebrate Christmas, for many years I went to a tree-trimming party hosted by my friend Joan Walsh in Oakland, later San Francisco. Joan had also worked at the *News & Review*. She moved on to write for *The Nation*, MSNBC, and CNN; her transition to New York City ended that holiday tradition, at least for me.

Although I donated many ornaments to the tree that Joan and her daughter Nora decorated over the years—a bamboo stork, an ersatz pickle, a tiny conga drum—I could never bring myself to part with this satellite. It seemed in some way a symbol of loneliness, out of place during the holiday season. Looking at it now reminds me how far I am from my old friends. David lives in Portland; Joan is in Harlem; I call Oakland home. We're each of us in our own orbit. Yet it's satellites like these that keep us connected, our affection expressed via social media posts and Zoom parties.

That I've held on to this ornament saddens me. It might otherwise be providing Joan and Nora a quantum of Christmas pleasure. Maybe it would remind them of me. They'd remember the night they unwrapped it, over plates of holiday ham and martinis: their initial mystification, my convoluted explanation, its placement on a high pine branch.

When I think that way, this satellite embodies a poignant paradox: Some objects don't really have stories, unless we give them away.

---

1. *It appears to be a crude replica of the GPS IIR, designed and built by Lockheed Martin.*

108 BELOVED OBJECTS

News Radio (Mini-) Swiss Army Knife
HOLLYWOOD, 1998

If you look me up on the IMDB website, you'll see that I have two credits for acting. One is for *Kidnap Party*, a 2012 film about which I know absolutely nothing. That's got to be another Jeff Greenwald—unless I actually *was* kidnapped, drugged, and compelled to perform in a hypnotized coma.

The *News Radio* credit, though, is another story.

It began with an email. The sender—a young Los Angeles casting director named Bonnie Zane—had read *The Size of the World*, and felt compelled to contact me.

"What you wrote about your brother's death was so moving," she said. "A few days before I left on a trip to Africa, actor Phil Hartman was murdered. The funeral was such a public affair... In some way, your book helped me deal with my grief." Phil Hartman, of course, was the beloved actor and male lead of *News Radio*—one of several popular TV sitcoms cast by Ms. Zane. Hartman had been shot and killed that May by his wife, who then committed suicide—sparing their two children.

Bonnie and I struck up a correspondence. She was fascinated by writing, and I longed to try acting. One afternoon, she called to tell me that a small speaking role was available on *News Radio*. "Get down here today," she told me, "and the part is yours."

I played "Security Guard." My two short scenes were with Patrick Warburton, best known today for his roles on *Seinfeld*, *The Tick*, and *A Series of Unfortunate Events*. Though I spoke just one line, my character had a dramatic arc—I would enter the scene soberly, but leave in tears of laughter. "You're actually *acting*," Bonnie reminded me.

It was so lovely to belong; to be part of that tight ensemble cast, even if just for 14 hours. To know I had comprehensive medical, full board, and a role to play. And like everyone lucky enough to stand in front of rolling cameras, I entertained a shimmering fantasy: Someone would see my performance, nudge their director friend and say, "Hey! See that security guard? He's *perfect* for our new series."

I'm ready to let that one go, along with this souvenir pocket knife. But as for my copy of the script for the *News Radio* episode titled "Jail" (Season 5, Episode 6)—autographed by the entire cast, minus Phil Hartman—that, I'm holding on to.

108 BELOVED OBJECTS

Copper, Brass & Bone Pipe with Leather Pouch

MAURITANIA, 1994

Choum is a small village in northern Mauritania—a country I have accurately described as "the world's largest cat litter box."

Multiple vehicle breakdowns had forced me to spend a day in Choum. It was blazing hot in that tiny outpost on the edge of the Western Sahara. I sat in the fly-blown shade of a Berber home—more a cement shack—watching a tall Black man iron a *djilaba*. He filled his mouth with water from the spout of an aluminum teapot, then sprayed it onto the white cotton robe with the industrial hiss of a steam cooker.

Sahimed, a round-faced Moorish trader, had accompanied me to Choum in a shared cab. Now he faced me on a threadbare carpet. He fished a handsome little smoking kit from his own robe, and nodded matter-of-factly in the man's direction. "That is one of the family's slaves," he announced.

"*Slave?*" I was flabbergasted. "Are you telling me that this family literally *owns* this man?"

"Yes. Slavery is now illegal in Mauritania," Sahimed said, a bit ruefully. "Since 1981, when the president banned it. But many people own slaves. It is the way." He shrugged. "And if free, where would they go?"

"You, too, own slaves?"

"Of course," said Sahimed. He rolled a cigarette, placed it in a brass holder and struck a match with his nail.

I stared at him in slack-jawed silence. Sahimed finished his cigarette, returned the pipe to its pouch and held out the kit. "For you." He placed his right hand over his heart, interpreting my revulsion as admiration. "A gift from a slave owner."

108 BELOVED OBJECTS

Sculpture/Painting with Pig Doll
LOS ANGELES, 1998

There's a photograph of me taken in 1981, in my studio on State Street in Santa Barbara. The image is blurred, because I'm dancing. I'm dancing because I'm 27 years old and deliriously happy. The walls are covered with art. I'm surrounded by my droll sculptural creations, my jubilant graphic output, hopeful of a future when my genius will be recognized. There was still time. It didn't bother me that I was living illegally in a small, shared studio in a downtown building and sleeping on a Goodwill couch. David, my studio mate, brought up takeout coffee in the morning. We worked all day, listening to Roxy Music and Talking Heads. Every hour was filled with inspiration, fabrication, conversation, romance.

There were many other artists in the Park Theater Building. I remember Michael Gonzales, a brilliant young painter who co-founded the annual Summer Solstice Celebration, and who would later die of AIDS. And Tim, a crazy person who always painted the same thing—a flat-topped mountain—and accused me, absurdly, of stealing his mail. But I had a good friend in Marsea Goldeberg: a brazen, hilarious, spontaneous woman who painted with a broad brush and bonked any number of our romping, oversexed cadre. She and I even got into a make-out session once. Marsea recoiled, complaining that my tongue was too big. It isn't. It's perfectly normal.

In 1983 I moved halfway across the world on a year-long fellowship, and never returned to Santa Barbara. Marsea and I stayed in touch. She married a fellow artist and moved to L.A., where she designed fabric prints for a while. She even opened her own gallery, which has become a success. And she was still painting—bold, colorful canvases featuring stuffed animals that she found in thrift stores.

I visited Marsea in 1998, a few years after she'd had her first child. Before I left, she gave me two stuffed animal paintings: one with a mounted lamb, the other with a pig. As my images of those happy years grow ever more blurred, and those vivid days of dervish dancing evaporate into mental line drawings, the lamb might bring back some happy memories. As for this pig... well... It reminds me of a big, pink tongue.

108 BELOVED OBJECTS

Gifts

Hello Kitty Toe Cleaner
JAPAN (GIFT; DATE UNKNOWN)

This was another gift from the peripatetic Mary Roach, acquired on her trip to JAXA, the Japanese space agency, during the writing of *Packing for Mars*. I doubt there is any connection between this device and the Japanese astronaut training program. Toe jam is one of the last things you want floating around you in zero gravity.

I've never used (or even opened) this between-the-toes cleaner, which looks like a repurposed double test tube scrubber. Maybe I should have—my feet have always been the least favorite part of my body, now more so than ever. I won't go into details.

There's really not much more I can say about this object. It was clearly designed with care, and the how-to illustration on the packaging is helpful. I hope it finds a happy home. Better with your feet than mine.

108 BELOVED OBJECTS

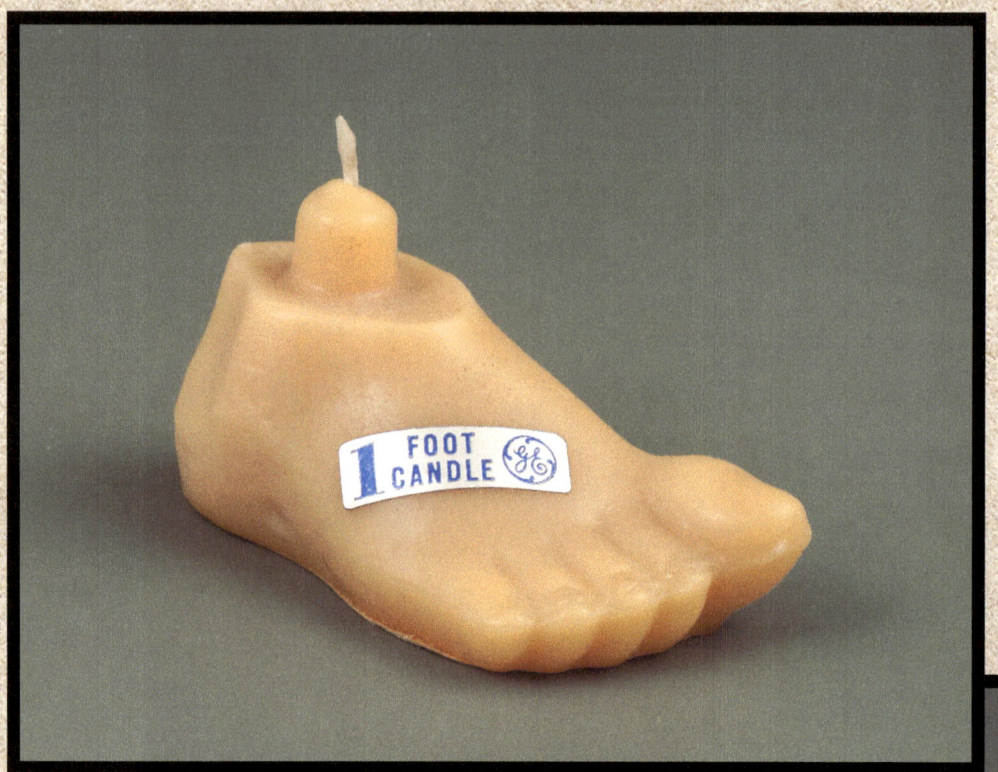
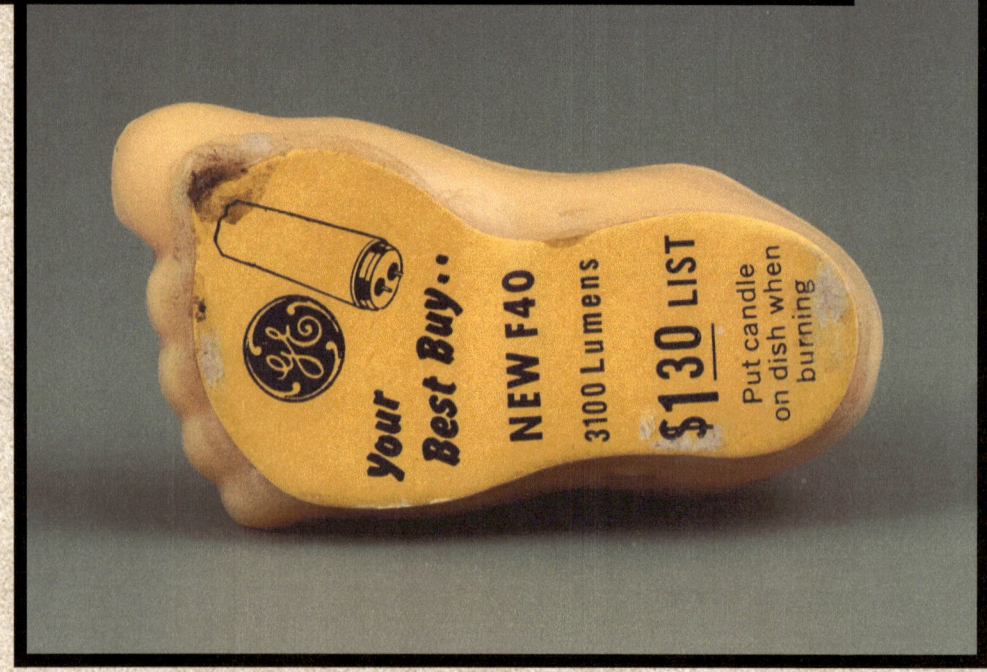

One Foot Candle

OAKLAND, 2016

This weird candle was a gift from Zena Kruzick, who photographed the objects in this book. Zena is an art appraiser and tribal art dealer, and knows how to make even humdrum items pop to life.

General Electric made these novelty feet to promote a new line of light bulbs. They're a pun on a "foot candle," a now defunct unit of light intensity. (One foot candle is the amount of light cast by a standard candle at a distance of one foot.) Bright daylight equals about 1,000 foot candles; the full moon, only 0.01. A typical computer display with a white background might be anywhere from 50 to 75 foot candles.

But GE does not make computer displays—or computers, for that matter. I wish my dad had known this would happen in the late 1960s, when the company hired him to head Northeastern sales for their data processing division. Back then, GE was making some of the first computers, modems, and fax machines. But when they sold their computer division to Honeywell in the 1970s, my father was fired. Seventeen years of service, thanks so much, don't let the door hit you on the way out.

Dad would have loved this candle. He delighted in physical puns of all kinds—from cocktail glasses belted with miniature jockstraps ("For Your High Balls") to the double entendre of Pussy Galore. But his sense of humor faded after GE let him go. He was nearly 50; back then, that was old. A part-time gig teaching data science at NYU wasn't enough to sustain him. Some of my last memories of my father see him sitting in our split-level rec room, staring at the TV, waiting for the phone to ring.

It never did. His red hair thinned, and went gray. His brightness faded. In mid-1983 I'd leave the U.S. for a two-year fellowship in Asia, and never see him again. (See *Kodak Beaker* story.)

Every September, on the anniversary of his death, I recite the kiddush in his memory. His portrait reflects the glow of a single foot candle—but never this one. I wish there had been less distance between us, Dad. Less distance, and more light.

108 BELOVED OBJECTS

Buddha Coin Bank
OAKLAND, 2008

I'm one of those people who has never been able to make any money. Real money, that is. Lord knows, I've tried. Endless ambitious projects and creations—from publishing six books to launching a stage show to founding what I believed would be an immensely successful non-profit organization. A travel podcast, group trips to Cuba and Nepal, freelance editing... I'm sure I'm leaving out a few dozen things.

But riches have eluded me—though I have been able to put a little away. It's not enough to buy even a small home here in Oakland, but it's enough to keep the hounds of debt at bay.

Colleagues who are not as self-critical as I point out that, in fact, I have managed to make a living as a freelance writer—no small achievement. The freedom seemed heady at first. Now that many of my friends are retiring with handsome pensions, I'm wondering who struck the better bargain.

But wealth and worldly comforts are notoriously transient. The only thing we truly have—and not for long—is our time, moment to moment, in this earthly realm. I've maintained some control over my own time, but not without continual episodes of doubt and anxiety. It's a slippery thing, devoting oneself to a career in the arts.

This Buddha coin bank was a gift to me on my 54th birthday—the day I outlived my father, who died a day short of his own. Though it's never held even a penny, it serves to remind me of a quote that Albert Einstein once wrote on his chalkboard at Princeton: "Not everything that can be counted, counts; and not everything that counts can be counted."

I don't know how many lessons I'll learn in this lifetime, or what I'll cherish or regret most in the end. But I hope I can find peace with the choices I've made, gratitude for what I've achieved, and satisfaction with the modest level of financial security I've been able to reach. That, for me, would pass for enlightenment.

Pall Mall Cigarette Pack
NEW YORK CITY, 1995

This object reveals much about the plasticity of memory—mine in particular.

In 1995, Kurt Vonnegut Jr. allowed me to interview him for my book-in-progress, *Future Perfect: How Star Trek Conquered Planet Earth*.

Approaching his midtown brownstone, I suddenly felt self-conscious about arriving empty-handed. Vonnegut had a huge influence on my life and writing, and he deserved a gift. But I didn't want to be late—and the only shop in sight was a florist. I assembled the most masculine-looking bouquet I could, and knocked at Vonnegut's door.

A housekeeper answered, Vonnegut himself close behind. He accepted the flowers, clearly flummoxed by my gesture, and asked the domestic to put them in a vase. We moved upstairs to his study and, surrounded by pillars of books, spoke about the strange global appeal of *Star Trek*. Vonnegut believed that the longing for community is as strong a human need as Vitamin C; there was little motivational difference, at core, between people who came together around *Star Trek*, the Grateful Dead, or even Charles Manson. Everyone, he said, just wants to belong.

Vonnegut chain-smoked during the entire interview. When he finished the pack, I asked if I might have it. He shrugged, flattened it out, and slipped it between the pages of a book I'd brought for him to sign: a 1st edition of *Slaughterhouse-Five*.

As we were wrapping things up, we heard the downstairs door open. "Hi, I'm home!" It was Vonnegut's wife, the photographer Jill Krementz, calling from below. Vonnegut appeared stricken. "Oh no," he said. "Her one-woman show in Chelsea is opening tonight, and I totally forgot." He shook his head in self-disgust.

A few seconds later, Jill called out again: "Sweetheart! Thank you for the flowers! They're beautiful!"

Kurt Vonnegut's face lit up with surprise and delight. "I love you," he whispered.

* * *

That is my memory of what happened. That is the story I've been telling myself, and my friends, for years. The problem is, I never bothered to read my own book (published in 1999) before launching into that touching and self-serving anecdote. After writing this chapter, though, curious about whether I'd included the story in *Future Perfect*, I opened the book. Here is a scene from that chapter, called *The Skin of a Toy Balloon*. Vonnegut and I had completed our interview, and left his study. He was giving me a tour of the brownstone. As we stopped in the dining room to look out into the back yard…

> *…There's a rustle in the hallway, and Vonnegut's wife—the photographer Jill Krementz—walks in. She has the wide-eyed, kinetic energy of someone who's just sat on a tack. Jill spies the bouquet of flowers, runs up to Kurt and throws her arms around his neck. "You are soooo sweet," she croons. She turns to me. "Tonight's my first gallery opening in twenty-two years." Back to Kurt: "It was so thoughtful of you to remember."*
>
> *Vonnegut narrows his eyes, his mouth a curve of ironic amusement. "They're from him," he confesses.*

That is what actually took place that afternoon in New York City. Isn't that interesting? Kurt Vonnegut Jr. did not panic; he did not take credit for the bouquet; he never told me he loved me. My brain, combing back through approximate facts, created a better story. And though I was disappointed to be chastised with the truth, I'm glad that I was.

But now, reflecting on all the stories in this book—on all the stories I've ever told—I wonder. All of my memories seem clear, accurate, visceral. But I wonder.

Earth, Moon & Stars

Crossing the Atlantic and Pacific Oceans on cargo ships during 1993 and 1994, my most absorbing companions were large sheets of paper: pilots' charts published by the Defense Mapping Agency. These red, white, blue, and gray ocean maps, created for ships' navigators, are peppered with circular glyphs called wind roses. Each circle has eight branches radiating outward—one for each of the main compass points. They tell the ship's pilot about the prevailing winds at that part of the sea, averaged from thousands of observations. A number inside each wind rose indicates how many days of the year that part of the ocean is completely calm; usually, not more than a few.

I was never completely calm during my transatlantic and transpacific crossings. Each journey held a fever of anticipation. On the far side of the Atlantic, docking in Senegal, I'd have my first real encounter with Africa; after crossing the Pacific, I'd at last be home after my 9-month circumambulation of the globe.

It was easy to get lost amid the wind roses and see my ocean voyages as abstractions, defined by maps, satellite navigation, and the glow of radar screens. What kept me anchored to reality was the scene outside, on deck. Days passed when the horizon stretched unbroken in every direction. The stars threw their ancient light on the high stacks of containers.

One evening aboard the Hapag-Lloyd *Bremen Express*, heading out to the fo'c'sle after drinking with the crew, I saw the sun set over the Pacific, precisely as the full moon was rising. I nearly lost my balance. For a brief, unforgettable moment it all came together: We are riding a sphere, turning in space amid uncountable stars, lit by the sun, partnered with the moon.

I was sauced. Sauced and philosophical. Being on a ship in the middle of the open sea for weeks on end is both meditative and terrifying, unnerving and blissful. How many, I wondered, have written about this paradox? Though you're restricted, the horizon appears infinite. Though limited in range, one is moving continuously forward, tracing a huge curve. Being on a ship, I perceived, is a perfect allegory for being on a planet.

And this planet, as Bucky Fuller made clear, *is* a ship. Every nation I'd visited on my odyssey (along with the 200-odd others I hadn't) lays cabined together on this sapphire sphere, rolling silently through the Milky Way. For a few score years—a trillionth of a wink in cosmic time—we get to share the stewardship of this tiny ark with 1.4 million other species: stinkbugs and elms, elephants and amanita, spider monkeys and sharks. From the Siberian phlox to the homeless guy hawking *The Street Sheet* on Market and 5th, we're passengers one and all—animated by a spark we cannot duplicate, have never found elsewhere, and struggle helplessly to define.

It's the only planet worth shit, I realized, *and I'm so in love with it I could scream*. And scream I did, a hoarse, drunken howl carried by the wind and pinballed ecstatically between imaginary wind roses.

108 BELOVED OBJECTS

Bamboo Souvenir "Camera"
FIJI, 2006

While I was at U.C. Santa Cruz—from 1975 to 1977—I lived in a house on Cayuga Street, splitting the $300/month rent with four (and sometimes as many as eight) roommates.

The core group included my best friend, Brian: a history major, rabble rouser, and rock climber who, despite his phobia of spiders, built a darkroom in our web-riddled basement. He taught me how to shoot, develop, and print black and white film. I loved it. Photography became a passion.

The grandmaster of photography at that time was, of course, Ansel Adams. His house sat on the rugged Monterey coast, not 50 miles south of Santa Cruz. One day I looked up his number, and dialed. "Come on down!" he said.

I slid my best 11x14 photos into a black cardboard portfolio, and fired up my Honda CB350. When I arrived, someone—his daughter Virginia, possibly—led me into the living room. There were a few other guests, and everyone seemed at home. I was handed a glass of red wine. It was a gorgeous home; the walls displayed Adams' best prints, and a cloudless Pacific sunset filled the living room's huge picture window.

Ansel, 74, occupied a comfortable chair. He motioned me over. "We're waiting for the green flash," he said with a grin. "I'm going to watch the sun until the right moment, and tell everyone when to look. I'm sacrificing my green flash," he confided, "for all of you."

Predictably, we didn't see the green flash. But my host agreed to look at the photos I'd brought. He was exceedingly gracious, and accepted one as a gift. He even gave me a small print of his own.

Those were the days. I was young and cheeky, and had a pretty high opinion of my talent. (One had better, starting out.) But now, when I look at the images I once showed Adams, I'm devastated. They may as well have been taken with this bamboo camera.

108 BELOVED OBJECTS

World Globe

UNKNOWN

My high school career was abysmal. I was bullied, my grades were awful, and the fact that I'd skipped 2nd grade meant I was a year younger than anyone else in my class.

College was a different story. Though it was a humble institution, Nassau Community College—located on the former Mitchel Air Force Base, with abandoned hangars serving as lecture halls and basketball courts—was a revelation. It was as if I'd swapped *Lord of the Flies* for Huxley's *Island*. An unprecedented self-confidence possessed me.

I loved my psychology classes, but my favorite subject was astronomy. Naively, I'd taken the class to learn the names of the constellations and other sexy facts about the moon and planets. But it was all math and physics. I well remember my midterm essay: "Calculating the Rotational Speed of Saturn from the Red Shift of its Rings."

Professor X was a gem: funny, challenging, a bit paunchy, adept. I was his best student. After our especially difficult midterm exam I was standing in the hallway, commiserating with my classmates about how tough and unfair the questions had been. X emerged, walked up, and placed a hand on my shoulder. "You're the first student," he declared, "to ever make a perfect score on that test." My classmates melted away, mumbling.

For the final, X gave us a bonus question which—if answered correctly—meant an automatic "A" for his class. "This is not a trick," Professor X announced. "So think very carefully before you answer: *How long does a day last on planet Earth?*"

Protests rang out across the room. What? It wasn't 24 hours? What did he mean, "a day?" On *this* planet Earth? "Long" measured in time, or miles?

"One day on planet Earth," he clarified. "Like today: Tuesday, May 12, 1973."

I got my "A" anyway, of course. But I'll never forget that deceptively simple question, and its surprising—but undeniably correct—answer. No one got it right. Not even me. If you do, this lovely lapis globe is yours.

108 BELOVED OBJECTS

Holy Water from the River Jordan
2012

"Human beings," as Tom Robbins mused in *Another Roadside Attraction*, "were invented by water as a device for transporting itself from one place to another."

One of the ideas behind *108 Beloved Objects* is that the act of "owning" something is often just permission to move it around. But I wonder if we actually "move" water, or if even thinking of water in those terms makes sense. We're not only made of water; water is made of us. I recently read that every drop of water contains molecules shared by every single person who has ever lived.

So if you want a personal connection with Buddha, Moses, Jesus, Joan of Arc, Galileo, Genghis Khan, Gandhi, Billie Holiday, and Bjork, just have a sip of water.

Can this be true?

It is—or very close. Every drop of water contains (more or less) 1.67×10^{21}, or 167,000,000,000,000,000,000 molecules. And a total of about 107,602,750,000 human beings have, thus far, been born. All of them have passed water through their bodies, and all of this water has comingled, in every waterway on Earth. (For more contemporary personages, less so. My drinking water may not yet hold a few trace molecules of Billie or Bjork.)

The point is, there's plenty of room for all of us in that drop, and a million generations to come. All the saints past, and all those as yet unborn.

So we had better think of *all* water as holy—not just the stuff in this jar. Which means I can give this Holy Water away without regret. My bathtub is full of the stuff.

108 BELOVED OBJECTS

Toy Story Alien Coin Bank
OAKLAND, CA, 1996

In 1993, I put together an unusual story for a newly launched magazine called *Wired*. Luminaries in the arts and sciences were asked to name the greatest new technological Wonders of the World. Their techno-wonders fell all over the map. They included the new generation of senior citizens (from author Douglas Coupland), talking primates (astronaut Mae Jemison), video games (Timothy Leary), and the self-cleaning garlic press (columnist Molly Ivins). My own contributions included ATMs and sunblock.

After the success of that first crowd-sourced feature, I pitched another story: *Where should aliens land first?*

Wired didn't bite, but the idea still fascinates me. The Earth is like the blind man's elephant. Any given landing site, from Paris to Pyongyang, would give our visitors an entirely different first impression of where they were—and who we are. Conversely, *their* choice of a site might be equally revealing. Imagine humanity's collective reaction if our first visitors touched down on the Acropolis, surrounded by Chinese tourists... or at the Peace Memorial in Hiroshima—to let us know they've been watching. Central Park might seem like a given to New Yorkers, but our guests might prefer a remote corner of the Gobi Desert.

Sometimes—especially while I'm traveling in the developing world—I reflect on the enormous accident of where I first showed up: in a Bronx hospital. It was a stroke of luck for which I have no explanation.

I like to think, and it may be true, that we all enter this world with the curiosity and innate optimism of *Toy Story*'s Pizza Palace alien. But so much depends on our landing coordinates. Some of us get to be astronauts or journalists; millions of others struggle to survive. Sometimes we're born under the smile of the Buddha. And sometimes we worship The Claw.

108 BELOVED OBJECTS

Carlsbad Caverns View Box
TIME AND PLACE UNKNOWN

During recent years, I have felt increasingly uncomfortable hiking in the woods. Not only in dense tropical rainforests, but even on the Manzanita-covered slopes of nearby Mount Tamalpais.

It seems I've developed agoraphobia: "A fear of crowded spaces or enclosed public places." Closets don't scare me, and neither do elevators. Traveling in a space capsule wouldn't be a problem. It's only when I'm immersed in a chaotic situation—be it on a densely wooded hillside, amid jostling cars in a parking lot, or at a crowded cocktail party—that I find myself breathless and agitated.

Maybe that's why I like caverns, with their illusion of limitless openness. Sometimes I let my imagination wander into this old souvenir view box, its blue-filtered slits shedding a peaceful pall onto the roughly sculpted walls. The box is small (only 3 inches wide) but very convincing. It reminds me of the View-Master® disks I loved as a kid, which transported me to other worlds.

I wish I could shrink myself to the size of a small ant and spend an afternoon inside this view box: writing in my journal, enjoying an aqua-tinted picnic, taking photographs, and gazing out at the brightly lit world beyond the cardboard frame.

In a way, I've sort of actually been there. Immersing myself within that tiny environment vividly recalls two very real places. The first is underwater, scuba diving through the filtered light of undersea caves in Belize, Hawaii, and Mexico. The second is inside the dimly lit altar rooms of Tibetan Buddhist monasteries, listening to the monks chanting as smoke from juniper incense curls through thin beams of penetrating sunlight.

Wow. This little souvenir is more than a view box. It's like the TARDIS, Dr. Who's deceptive time and space machine: tiny when viewed from the outside, but infinitely spacious within.

108 BELOVED OBJECTS

Dzo Bell

DEBUCHE, NEPAL 2008

Sometimes, in Kathmandu, I shut off all my senses but one. Closing my eyes, folding my hands on my lap, ignoring the panoply of aromas and odors that perfume every inch of Nepal, I open up my ears.

The spectrum of sounds has changed radically since my first visit, in 1979. Back then the soundtrack was temple bells and barking dogs, the slip and grind of bicycle rickshaw chains, children shouting, the thin report of hammers on brick and iron. Today it's car horns and generators, two-stroke motorbikes, the clang of shutting gates. And dogs, of course. And hammers, always.

Trekking north on the rocky trail toward Everest Base Camp, I didn't dare close my eyes—one wrong step can send you tumbling into the valley below (see *Nikomat EL* chapter). But the audio landscape of the Himalaya, even in 2008, was as pure as it had been during my first trek to the Khumbu region in 1983. The steady wash of the Imja Kola river; wooden prayer wheels creaking in a rustic temple; stones rattling down a glacial slope; and the hollow metallic clang of yak bells. Not yaks, actually, but *dzo*: a hybrid between yaks and lowland cattle, grazing in a trailside pasture.

As I crossed their path, the animals raised their heads to study me, mouths still chewing. Their horns were long and sharp, but the eyes below them were kind. The shepherds beckoned to me in greeting: *Namasté! Aunos!* I stepped into the field to meet them—and got a closer look at one of the bells, hanging loosely from one dzo's neck.

Much of what happens in Nepal makes no rational sense. The moment I saw this bell I knew that no anecdote or written description—nothing short of a show-and-tell—would properly convey my cognitive dissonance. So after a friendly chat with the shepherds, I made my proposition. The shepherds burst out laughing. Buy a dirty old bell? Then they nodded. From their point of view, the behavior of we parka-clad foreigners—wheezing in wonder through their villages—seldom made sense.

I will never know when, why, or how this worn tin bell, untied from the thick neck of a Khumbu dzo, ended up emblazoned with an equally worn NASA decal. Was it put there by a visiting astronaut? A NASA engineer? Had Buzz Lightyear trekked past these farm animals, and gifted a few stickers to the shepherds?

Before my first visit to Nepal, I thought there was an explanation for everything. These days, I'm grateful for the gift of unsolved mysteries. This battered bell, with its space-age sticker, is a true riddle—an uncanny nod to my life as a trekker, both stellar and terrestrial.

108 BELOVED OBJECTS

Weather Watch

NATURAL BRIDGES, KENTUCKY, 1999

Three bookstore readings had been scheduled on the Kentucky tour for *Future Perfect,* my book about *Star Trek* in global culture. One of them was in Lexington, at 7 p.m. The morning and afternoon of that day were free. Though I'd initially hoped to picnic with my "handler"—the very attractive woman who'd picked me up at the airport the previous evening —I was put off by the question she'd asked me at breakfast: "Have you accepted Jesus Christ as your lord and savior?"

I have not, and so decided instead to rent my own car and explore Natural Bridges State Resort Park, an hour's drive east.

I have few clear memories of that book tour, or even of the huge sandstone bridge that gives the state park its name. What I do recall is that, as I was pulling onto Interstate 64, a song came on the radio. Played on a banjo, the tune was unmistakable: It was the theme from *Star Trek,* hillbilly-style.

I was so blown away, it's fair to say my tail went missing.

Those sorts of strange blessings and signs used to fall steadily upon me. These days, not as much. Why is that? Was I simply more attuned to them before? Or is it because, my fearless youth behind me, I'm no longer as entertaining to whatever divine forces, Judeo-Christian or otherwise, serve as our puppet masters? Have they simply turned their attention elsewhere?

That defeatist point of view could, of course, be reversed at any moment. My weather eye is still open for miracles.

108 BELOVED OBJECTS

Silver Seahorse (or Dragon) Container
BALI, 2005

Bali is all about water. Ponds smothered in lotus flowers and gardenias; streams pitching from the ambrosial urns of stone goddesses; waterfalls along stone walls covered with butterflies and fronds.

I was used to being wet. I'd arrived in Bali after spending a week on the Indonesian island of Bunaken. The assignment came from Seacology, a nonprofit dedicated to protecting island ecosystems. They'd hired me to write about three of their community-based projects in Indonesia. These included a heroic effort to restore the island's coral reefs, many of which had been destroyed by cyanide or dynamite fishing.

The bath-warm waters surrounding Bunaken conceal some of the most beautiful dive sites in the world. Three marine systems converge in that region, supporting a dense web of marine life full of biological surprises. Shortly before my visit, in fact, a new species of seahorse had been discovered by a local dive master named Henche Pontoh; the creature, *Hippocampus pontohi*, now bears his name.

That's probably why this odd metal seahorse, which I found in a Balinese antique shop, caught my eye. At least I think it's a seahorse. Or maybe a dragon? And why are humanoid figures riding on its back, clinging to its mane and tail? It's either a scene from a local myth, some kind of tribal object, or a flight of pure imagination. (It's also an unlikely container, splitting apart at the middle.)

Is it old, or new? It's often hard to tell about things you find in Bali. One afternoon in Ubud, strolling through the Monkey Forest, I wandered down a flight of steps to the river. To my left, on a rocky outcrop overlooking the raging, muddy torrent, sat two gigantic carved stone lizards. Weathered and covered with moss, they stared down at the rushing water. I was enchanted by these reptiles, convinced they were ancient ruins—until I saw the sculptor's signature, dated 1997.

My intentions for this seahorse are unclear. In 2005 it was meant as a gift, but for whom? Clearly, I never succeeded in giving it away. It embodies a kind of fecund island mystery. I suspect it may still have some stories to tell me. So this is a hard object to let go of. But aren't they all?

108 BELOVED OBJECTS

Star Trek Communicator Badge
LOS ANGELES, 1997

A quick tap on the brass and silver badge—"*Beam me up!*"—followed by the sparkle of the *USS Enterprise*'s atomic fax machine. For those of us who grew up with *Star Trek*, the transporter's twinkling trill is as familiar as the fizz of Alka-Seltzer®.

When the show that Gene Roddenberry originally pitched as a "*Wagon Train* to the stars" premiered in 1966, humans were racing to the Moon. Rocket ships—with astronauts aboard—were blasting off every few months. Kids like me (I was 12 at the time) fully expected to visit orbiting hotels (as per *2001: A Space Odyssey*) and bounce around in the Moon's 1/6 gravity. All of us would float weightless in space; a lucky few might even walk on Mars. Space would be our playground.

We didn't get any of that.

What we *did* get, though, are *Star Trek*'s gadgets. For the past 50 years, companies like IBM, Apple, Xerox, and SpaceX have been working to manifest the technology that their young engineers saw on that show. Warp-drive and teleportation remain elusive; but communicators, PADDs, and talking computers are here. Even Amazon's drone delivery is a Flintstones-level nod to the *Enterprise* replicator.

I've been a *Star Trek* fan since the beginning. But the truth is, I'm not much of a gadget guy. I just replaced my old flip phone—with a newer old flip phone. What my young heart desired from that famous starship was not materialistic: It was a sense of community, and the possibility of far-flung adventures. I wanted to emulate the self-confidence of Kirk, the humanistic curiosity of Picard, the cool logic of Spock, the nobility of Worf.

Even as a grown-up, the fantasy stuck. When I bought this handsome communicator badge at the Paramount Pictures gift shop, I imagined it would confer upon me a kind of knighthood; that by wearing it I'd elevate my personal rank to Starfleet level, and be recognized by kindred spirits as a farsighted member of a pan-galactic cuddle puddle.

I guess it kind of works, if you wear it to Comic-Con on a well-tailored blue Starfleet jersey. On an REI fleece vest at Peet's coffee, not so much.

108 BELOVED OBJECTS

Sumo Wrestler

JAPAN, 1984

During my first visit to Japan, a sensation erupted in the sumo world. The Hawaiian-born Konishiki—then only 20 years old—was defeating Japan's best wrestlers, and threatening to become the first non-Japanese-born person to attain the rank of *ozeki*: the penultimate title in the sumo pyramid. Weighing in at 606 lbs., Konishiki could knock over his opponents with ease. His nickname was "The Dump Truck."

There's something deliciously peaceful about watching a *honbasho* (sumo tournament). The vast energy and precise strategy of the combatants is belied by their enormous weight, which can give the battle—to a naïve observer—the sad hilarity of a freak show. That wasn't my experience. I only attended one match, in Kyoto, and it seemed simultaneously majestic and balletic to me.

After the bouts, I waited in the vestibule with dozens of other fans, hoping for the chance to to pat Konishiki's haunch—or whatever part of his voluminous physique I could reach—as he lumbered back to the "stable." He waddled by, smiling, his flesh undulating from our congratulatory slaps.

A year later, my friend Nick and I watched a monsoon storm coalesce above the Kathmandu Valley. The clouds were huge, pale, and bulbous, and as a pair of them tussled, I told Nick of the sumo bouts I'd watched in Japan. Here, though, the warriors were weightless.

"Nothing could be further from the truth," Nick said in surprise. "Clouds are the heaviest things around. Imagine how much water is in that thunderhead: millions of gallons! At eight pounds a gallon, your average thunderhead probably weighs half a million tons."

Some people believe science is the antithesis of magic; a little knowledge makes the miraculous seem drab. Stars are nuclear furnaces; rainbows appear through the diffraction of water droplets. Love is a chemical reaction; our lovers themselves evolved from apes. And a drifting white cloud weighs as much as a container ship.

Do you see that one up there? It looks like a cherry-blossom tree.

108 BELOVED OBJECTS

Dance Wax
OAKLAND, 1997

While many white people dance badly, I'm especially clumsy on my feet. Dancing in any coordinated way, from salsa to waltzing, eludes me. But when a friend offered me this dance wax, I eagerly accepted. I mean, just look at it! Coolest. Box. Ever.

Though this package is from 1950, dance wax is still sold on Amazon. "We have a new hardwood dance floor and everyone complained it was too sticky for dancing," said Ron @ Tacoma Elks Lodge #174 in his five-star review. "We bought the … Dance Wax and simply shook some out of the can onto the floor. Now everyone loves our dance floor. I am glad I bought the whole case!"

Even a case of the stuff would not help me. In my fantasy, this object will be gifted to the well-known astrophysicist Neil deGrasse Tyson—who is also an accomplished ballroom dancer. Maybe Tyson would, in return, agree to have lunch with me sometime.

I'd give him an earful. Tyson (who once appeared on *Dancing with the Stars*) supports the idea that Pluto is a "dwarf planet." Pluto, he claims, does not deserve to be ranked among the "real" planets of our solar system. I oppose that ridiculous view. It's like saying that penguins aren't really birds, because they don't fly. Or that the element francium, with a half-life of only 22 minutes, should give up its place on the periodic table.

Pluto is not only a planet, it's one of the coolest planets. Its existence was first deduced in the 1780s, when it was known as "Planet X." Pluto itself was discovered in 1930—and now, thanks to the probe New Horizons' 2015 flyby, we've seen it up close. There's a beautiful valentine heart on its surface; the landscape looks like the Dakota Badlands, but super icy. So Pluto may be small, but, like Danny DeVito, it's badass.

Best of all? On the surface of Pluto, with its low mass and gravity, I'd weigh only 10.2 pounds. It's the only planet in the solar system where even I could be light on my feet.

108 BELOVED OBJECTS

Moon Landing Commemorative Plaque
PLAINVIEW, 1969

At 10:56 p.m. EST on July 20th, 1969, Apollo 11 astronaut Neil Armstrong stepped onto the Moon. I was a peach-fuzzed 15-year-old, obsessed with the space program. My closet was stacked with "collectors" copies of *Life* and *Time* which—like every other all-American magazine—had cheered on the Space Race since the days of Project Mercury.

What had gotten me most excited about the final frontier was the film *2001: A Space Odyssey*. The dark, mystical expanse of outer space evoked in me a powerful wanderlust —as if my inner state of alienation would find its perfect home in that lonely realm.

The 13" black-and-white TV in my bedroom flickered as Armstrong descended the narrow ladder leading from the hatch of the LEM (Lunar Excursion Module) to the Moon's dusty surface. Though I'd never had a drink (unless you count a few sips of Manischewitz at Passover), I had sneaked a split of cheap champagne for this occasion. When Armstrong said "I'm going to step off the LEM now," I popped the cork.

You can easily find the video of those first steps: grainy images that roughly capture the ladder, the LEM, and Armstrong's bungled first words: "That's one small step for man," said he, "one giant leap for mankind." No one who heard the quote in real time thought it made much sense. Armstrong actually paused after the first phrase, possibly realizing that he'd blown it: He had meant to say, "That's one small step for *a* man." So the first human emotion felt on the Moon may well have been embarrassment.

Three years later, I wrangled an assignment to cover the launch of Apollo 17—the last Moon mission—for my college newspaper. It was my first assignment, and it was awesome. The Saturn V rocket, tall as a 36-story building, lifted off from Cape Kennedy at 12:33 a.m., torching the Florida sky with a white-orange glow. Seabirds scattered in a panic, and the thunder of the five flame-spewing engines dropped me to my knees.

Those astronauts spent more than three days on the Moon. They had a fucking *car*! But by the time of their mission, few people bothered to watch the launches or moonwalks anymore, let alone varnish First Day of Issue stamps to chunks of wood.

I once asked futurist Arthur C. Clarke if there was something he had failed to predict. "I never dreamed we would go to the Moon," he said, "and then stop."

The Moon shots were a fabulous, wildly expensive, symbolic, patriotic adventure—but though I thought I'd live to see the all-you-can-eat fried clam buffet at the Howard Johnson in orbit, I'm out of luck. In the end, a total of 12 men walked on the Moon—and all I got was this lousy plaque.

108 BELOVED OBJECTS

Nikomat EL Camera
SAN FRANCISCO, 1976

This beauty was my first serious camera. I bought it slightly used from my friend Bill Parker. Parker is a sculptor who creates artworks with light, electricity, and plasma; he was a colleague of mine when I worked at the San Francisco Exploratorium in 1974 and 1975. Bill had bought it in Japan, so it's called a "Nikomat" instead of a "Nikkormat"—I'm not clear exactly why.

Four years later, in September 1979, I was trekking alone in Nepal's Annapurna range. This was long before the road was put in; today you can drive all the way from Pokhara to Tibet, and onward to Beijing. But back in those days, the trail was so steep and narrow that you had to watch every step. Many trekkers hired local porters, sometimes even donkeys. Not me. At 25—muscular and fit—I scorned the use of porters. No need; my backpack weighed only 50 lbs.

I had left the hilltop village of Ulleri, and was quickly and confidently descending a long, precipitous procession of smooth slate steps. It was early in the morning, and they were slick with dew. The trail, following a ridge, turned sharply. Suddenly, I slipped. My body pitched forward, off the edge of the trail, the mass of my backpack plunging me head first into a V-shaped gap between two huge boulders.

This Nikomat was hanging around my neck by a black leather strap. It swung into the V before me. My head followed right behind. The shallow dent at the top of the camera is the exact spot where my chin slammed into the prism casing. The sturdy camera, wedged into the V like a brick, prevented my skull from being crushed like a walnut.

I was briefly trapped, nearly upside down, in the narrow crevasse. Two passing Sherpas pulled me out. My left arm was scraped up and bleeding, but that was all. One of my rescuers used his fist to hammer the camera out from below. Aside from the bruised prism casing, the only other damage was a shattered UV filter.

The Nikomat still worked perfectly, and continued to serve as my main professional camera for the next 15 years. The shallow dimple was a continual reminder that it had once literally saved my life. It's very unlikely that my current camera—an iPhone 7—would do me the same favor.

108 BELOVED OBJECTS

Apple iPod (2nd Generation, Touch Wheel, 20 GB)

OAKLAND, 2002

Driving north from Oakland in 2001, I saw a billboard advertising the first iPod. Though I had no idea what I was looking at, I remember having a strange feeling that, whatever it was, it would change the world.

It certainly changed mine. Music fuels my writing— and in the early 1980s, my Asia packing lists included a hefty boom box and a soft case holding two dozen cassette tapes. (These were not the heaviest things I carried; my Smith Corona typewriter filled half of my backpack.) Within the decade, the tapes were replaced with CDs. But still.

Suddenly, none of that baggage was necessary. The number of songs I could load onto this iPod was virtually unlimited. A plug-in speaker completed the kit. From that point on, it became impossible to keep up with the overabundant music on my devices—and so it remains today.

But the universal availability of any music, at any time, came at a cost: the death of anticipation. I used to love cycling up to Telegraph Avenue and rambling through the used CD bins at Amoeba and Rasputin, experiencing the giddy endorphin rush of finding that obscure Stan Getz or Van Morrison recording. Today, like everything else, *Boozoo Hully Gully* is just a mouse-click away.

What fascinates me about our 21st-century devices (and the Internet as a whole) is that none of the sci-fi authors I read (and I read a lot of sci-fi) predicted them. The only one who came close was H.G. Wells: "A World Encyclopedia," he said in a 1937 radio broadcast, "no longer presents itself to a modern imagination as a row of volumes printed and published… but as a sort of mental clearing house for the mind; a depot where knowledge and ideas are received, sorted, summarized [and] compared… This Encyclopedic organization need not be concentrated now in one place; it might have the form of a network [that] would constitute the material beginning of a real World Brain."

Wow. Right? I'll tell you what *I* wish I had predicted: that I should put my money where my music was. When I bought my first iPod in June of 2002, Apple stock was $1.50 a share. *"Regrets? I have a few…"*

108 BELOVED OBJECTS

Lighthouse Lager
BELIZE, 2003

November isn't supposed to be the rainy season in Belize, but the sky fell every day. We slept to the patter of drops on the skylights over our bunks, and breakfasted to the report of rain on the tarp above the dining table. There was always a storm on the horizon, in every direction. Every now and then the sun emerged between distant clouds and pierced the sea, a jeweler's lamp through an emerald. Then the colors faded, the sun vanished, and the rattle of raindrops on *Ananda*'s deck grew like distant applause, building in intensity as the monotonous parade of clouds approached.

A magazine had sent me to Belize. I had a story to write, about sun-washed islands, and the rain was not helping.

"The trick," E. suggested as we popped Lighthouse beers and studied the horizon, "is to surrender. Embrace the non-eventfulness of the trip. It doesn't have to be *about* anything."

A show about nothing, as George Costanza described *Seinfeld*. Even the most pedestrian of life's events—renting a car, buying soup, installing a showerhead—can be a vehicle for storytelling. But was that possible in Belize? What is the line between a story being about nothing in particular, and being about nothing at all? A story has to have a beginning, middle, and end—doesn't it?

Turns out, it doesn't. I composed a story about the rain and the sea and the Belizeans we drank with on the islands; I shared their stories about slavery and hurricanes, shark sightings, festivals, and pirates. And yes—I even got a Seinfeld reference in there. In the end, it worked.

Best of all, during the writing process, I learned a larger lesson: The individual stories that illustrate our lives might seem like stories about nothing—but our lives themselves are always about something.

108 BELOVED OBJECTS

Moon Rocket Bottle Opener
OAKLAND (DATE UNKNOWN)

This rocket, like the communications satellite on pages 68-69, may have been a gift from my friend David McCutchen, who shares my love for spaceships and dinosaurs. It's surprisingly heavy, and one can easily miss the bottle opener attachment at the bottom. Years of display in the direct sun on my kitchen windowsill has faded the once bright paint, and the traces that remain look like they were applied by a child.

The playful model reminds me of the afternoon and evening I spent interviewing astronaut Buzz Aldrin in 1999, the 30th anniversary of the first lunar landing. I met the vital, blue-eyed astronaut—he was then 69—in his Wilshire Boulevard apartment, and as an opening gambit, asked him which questions he was most sick of.

"Don't ask me 'how it felt' to walk on the Moon," the Apollo 11 Lunar Module Pilot cautioned. "I'm sick of that question. It's *unanswerable*."

About an hour into our conversation, Aldrin warmed up and began to tell me how it felt *after* walking on the moon. "Once we came home, we were in quarantine aboard the U.S.S. Hornet," he said, "in case we'd picked up any moon bugs. We were there for three weeks. During that time, the Hornet crew brought us newsreels of people all over the world, watching the moon landing together. Big crowds in Times Square, Paris, Tokyo, Brazil. It was a global event, an experience shared by millions of people around the world.

"I remember Neil (Armstrong) turning to me and saying, 'We missed it!' And it was true. Every person I've met, for the past 30 years, has told me exactly where they were at the moment we walked on the moon. We were *doing* it, but we didn't share in that experience. Neil, Michael, and I were actually up there—but we missed the whole thing."

108 BELOVED OBJECTS

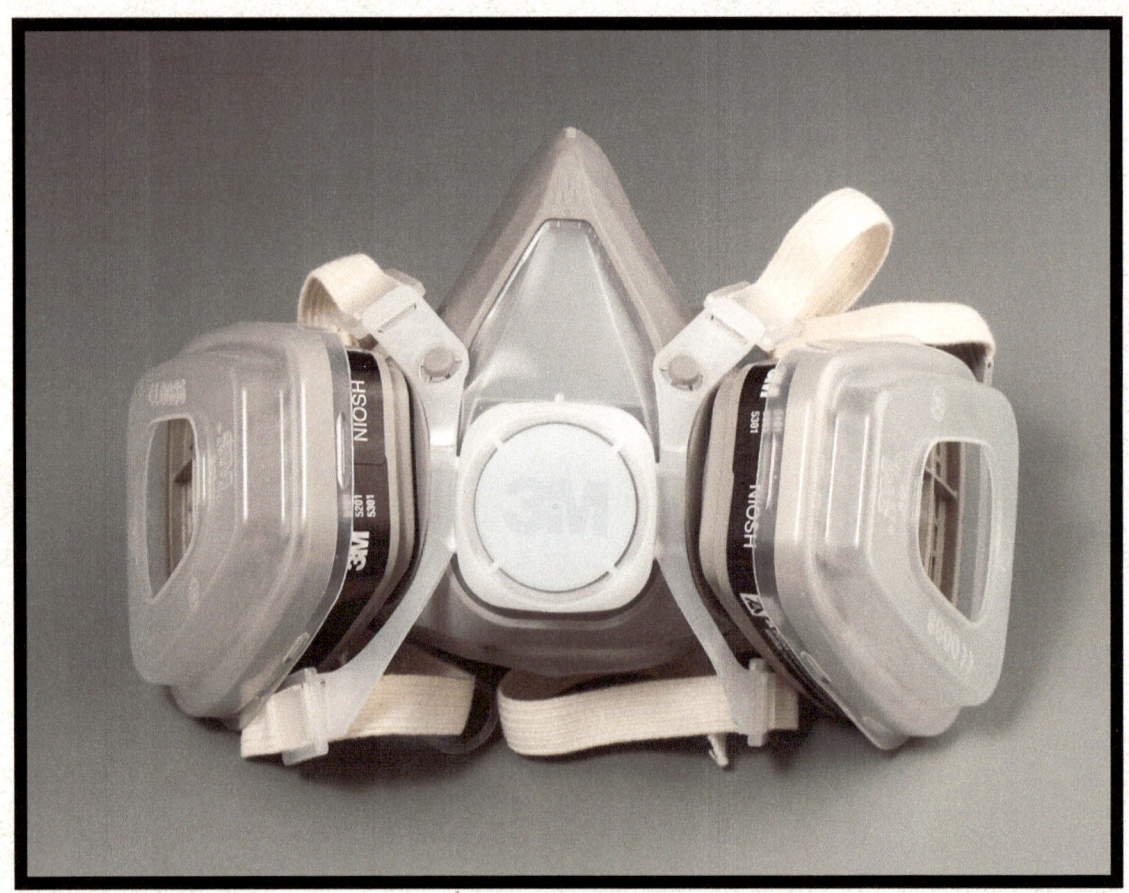

3M Dual Cartridge Respirator
OAKLAND, 2018

A small airplane waited on the tarmac in Alice Springs, bound for Darwin. My connection from Sydney had been late, and though the twin-engine aircraft had started down the runway, the pilot stopped for me and lowered the steps. By the time I boarded, hauling my satchel, I was dripping sweat. The only free seats were in the rear. Grateful, still pulsing with adrenaline, I dropped into the nearest one.

All 16 of the other passengers turned around to look at me. One woman, toward the front, half-stood. "You're a Yankee, aren't you?" I nodded. "Where from?"

"Oakland, California."

"Well, mate—your town is on fire." She held up a newspaper. On the page was the now famous black-and-white photograph of the Claremont Hotel, its venerable edifice framed by a backdrop of flames. This was October, 1991.

An artist couple I knew, Janet and Richard, lost their home in the Oakland Hills firestorm. They were at a San Francisco beach when it occurred, with only the clothes on their backs. Everything was consumed. Janet's father had built the house, which held her life's work in experimental sound recording. Richard lost all of his paintings. Furniture, clothes, jewelry, keepsakes, bicycles, dishware—all gone.

When I returned from Australia the following week, we visited the site together. Of the house, only the foundation remained. A hardened silver pool was once a refrigerator; a twisted ball of glass their computer monitor. In the charred garage, a sculptural mass of wiry metal, filled with ashes, had been a suitcase. It held the love letters that Janet's parents exchanged during World War II, when her father was a pilot and her mother a nurse. "We kept them in a suitcase," Janet explained, "so we could save them first if there was an earthquake."

After the fire, Janet and Richard did something remarkable. Having lost all of the material objects that defined them, they looked at their non-material lives. Starting from zero, they decided to reinvent themselves. Their first question was, "Do we stay married?" They did—and rebuilt their lives from there.

Twenty years later, wildfires are pandemic in the wooded world. As I write this, Australia itself is burning. The Amazon is in flames. And fires visit California every year, engulfing thousands of acres. The smoke in Oakland is sometimes so bad that we need filtration masks. For me, I've discovered, the smaller, lighter N95 face masks are good enough.

Fire is so terrifying. And yet somehow, cleansing. Sometimes I wish, if only for a nanosecond, that a fire would take all of my own possessions, while sparing my life. Thousands of slides from scores of trips; journals dating back to 1970; letters from my brother, and past loves; my stereo and television and bass; every worldly possession described in this book, and a thousand other objects as well. Everything I have ever had the compulsion to save.

108 BELOVED OBJECTS

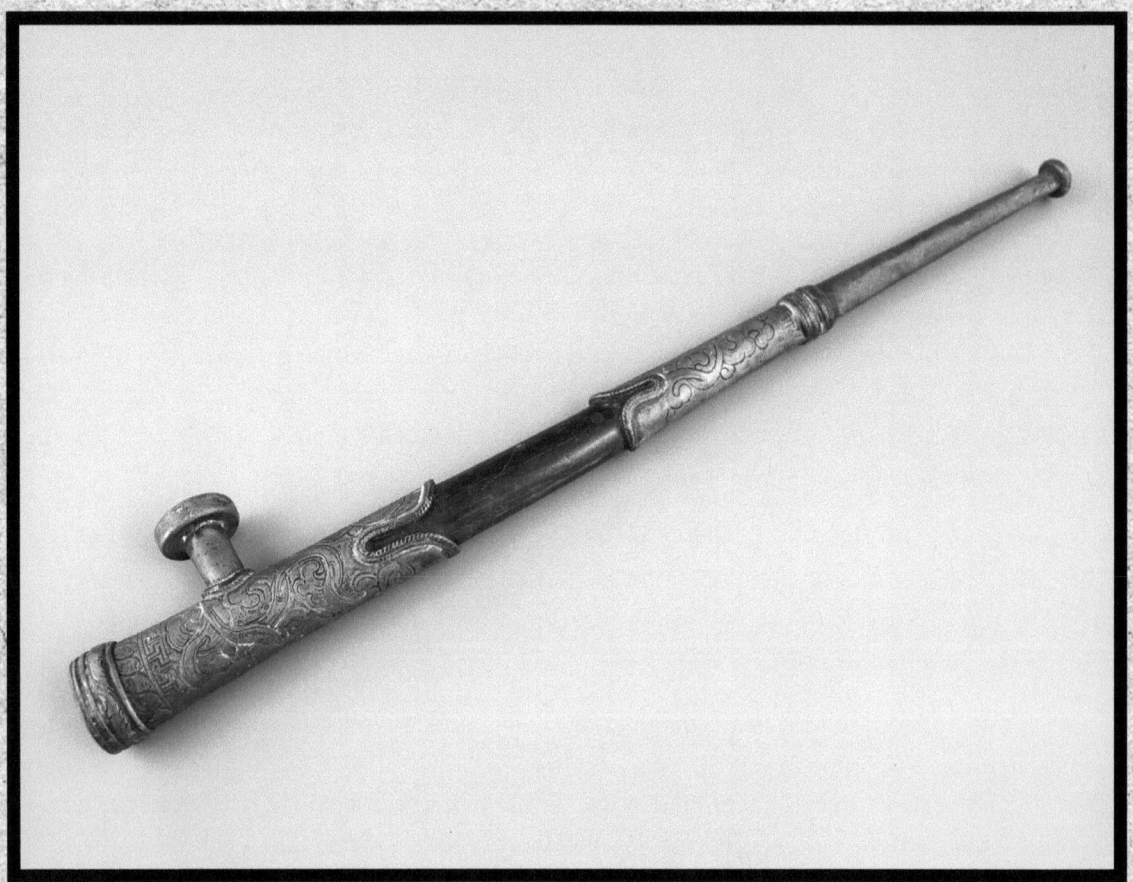

Silver & Bone Tibetan Pipe
TIBET, 1987

I never smoked opium while in Tibet, nor knew anyone who did. But these Sino-Tibetan pipes were once in wide use. This one was a gift from a friend in Lhasa.

The Nepal/Tibet border opened to tourism in 1985, making the long-forbidden plateau much more accessible. A couple of years later, two friends and I took a taxi northeast from Kathmandu, walked across a river to the Chinese customs post, and made our way to Lhasa. During the next several months we trekked across rough, high-altitude aeries that were simultaneously vast, spectacular, and monotonous.

During one multiday slog through a wide, rocky valley pocked with fallen *gompas* (Buddhist monasteries) that had been destroyed during the Cultural Revolution, the three of us tried an experiment. We had between us a few tabs of LSD, and we cut them into quarters. Every morning and afternoon we each ate one of the fragments. The mild "micro-dose" kept us in a state of benign fascination.

Late one afternoon, we rounded a bend and saw in the near distance a magnificent site: The shell of a once majestic Tibetan gompa, its broken stone walls painted red, ochre, and white, loomed on the valley floor far ahead of us. The low sun illuminated the ruin like a spotlight. I focused my Nikon, took a photograph, and walked on.

I hadn't gone two steps when I looked at the gompa again. The light had changed dramatically. I took another picture. A minute or so later, the sun's angle—and the light—shifted again. The scene was otherworldly, and I had to capture it.

Months later, I processed my Tibet film and loaded the slides into a projector. There were about 70 photographs of the gompa. They all looked exactly the same.

Far from feeling foolish, it made me wistful. I wanted to remember what I'd seen when I'd taken those shots. It was as if I had roused myself in the middle of the night to scrawl down a hilarious joke from a dream, only to wake in the morning and read, "Buy the dog a zipper!"

Opium dreams, LSD visions; everything we see, everyone we love, every moment we experience. We can't hold on to a single frame of it. That's what the Buddha taught. It's a harsh smoke.

Love

She was sitting outside the hostel in Delphi: a petite woman in a feathery blouse, playing an actual silver flute. Blonde hair cascaded down her shoulders. It was 1979, and even though eight years had passed since the release of *Blue*—and with it, the song *A Case of You*—I was still in love with Joni Mitchell. Or at least the idea of finding a woman like Joni Mitchell, somewhere. Ideally, of course, in Greece.

I sat nearby, opened my journal, and began sketching. She put down her flute and watched me for a while. "You are an artist?" And back then, honest to God, I was.

Linda was French Canadian, her eyes the greenish-blue of a backlit wave. We packed a picnic of bread and feta cheese, *retsina* and a cucumber, and carried a blanket up a nearby hill, on the outskirts of the ancient city. After a few long swallows from the *bota* bag we were high enough to giggle at the goats grazing around us, and a few minutes later, drunk enough to kiss, the way you kiss when you're 25 and traveling alone and lying on a thin blanket in a meadow filled with wildflowers, bees, and goat shit.

For two days, we were inseparable. We explored the ruins, consulted the Delphic oracle, and made clumsy love in my mummy bag in a room with three other people pretending not to notice.

Then, we got the urge for going. She to Turkey, myself to Nepal.

On May 17th, we took the bus back to Athens. I know, because I began a new journal that day. We bought coffee and pastries at a café near the station.

"I made something for you," Linda said. Somehow, during our few moments apart, she had found some soft leather and lace and sewed me a new passport holder. It was embroidered with flowers and had a long, narrow leather strap. She leaned toward me, her breath on my mouth, and hung it around my neck.

We kissed again, this final time feeling like the first. She wrote down an address where I could reach her, later, once we'd both returned to our homelands. We swore we'd stay in touch, write often, meet again, maybe rent a flat together, the dark-haired artist from California and the beautiful Canadian musician. Children were not out of the question.

We never saw each other again.

I still have the leather pouch somewhere, the neck strap broken, the tiny white flowers both joy and admonition. It is impossible to hold it in my hands without tasting Linda's breath, smelling goats, and remembering how, when I stood up to bid her farewell, I brushed the crumbs of a cheese Danish off my shorts.

So much love, so many objects. But as always, it is the story—itself an ever-changing apparition—that we never want to misplace. And maybe that's why the objects we hold onto are so important: They are the seal on the envelope, the lock on the box holding Schrödinger's cat. Our stories are whatever we want them to be. The object is proof that they happened—not how they happened.

Twenty years from now, that little hide pouch will still transport me back to our days in Delphi, and that hormone-drugged afternoon on the hill. But if Linda herself were to cross my path tomorrow, I wouldn't have a clue. I wonder: Would she? And did I leave her with anything, except forgotten promises?

It's love's illusions I recall. If not for this object, nothing of those days—no evidence or impartial witness—would remain.

108 BELOVED OBJECTS

Dancing Goddess
NEPAL, 1984

I'm not a fan of porn. It's the erotic figures found in Hindu and Buddhist paintings and sculpture that turn me on. There's something about those beatific devotional female deities—they're among the wonders of the world.

There are so many statues for sale in Nepal that trying to choose the "right" one can be maddening. In fact, as you may know, I wrote a book about this: *Shopping for Buddhas*. That tale was set in 1988. But during earlier trips to Asia I was less meditative, and more on the lookout for comely representations of the full-figured maidens I'd seen portrayed across the subcontinent—from the cave murals in Sri Lanka to the acrobatic lovers of Khajuraho.

In 1984, I couldn't afford a "perfect" sculpture. So, I combed the statuary shops for artworks that were *almost* perfect, save for a fatal flaw, and so might be purchased at a deep discount.

This dancing goddess (I think of her as a goddess, though she's probably simply a dancer) looked wonderful in the store window… but her waist is not fitted properly. The top half of her body rattles around in the hips and is never poised quite right. Still, I was thrilled and grateful to possess this artwork. I displayed her in my hallway, draped with the glass bead necklaces described elsewhere in this book.

I'm older now, and my own body is coming loose. A spinal staph infection hospitalized me for a week, and earned me my first (temporary) handicapped parking placard. I'm not the only one with issues: My lover has a growth on her lower eyelid that may or may not be cancerous; my business partner was recently hospitalized for a rare heart condition; and my beautiful paramour thinks she may be a close candidate for hip replacement surgery.

It's ironic. I'm at a point in my life when I can afford top-tier works of art. But I'm in love with flesh-and-blood women who—especially if they're in my age group—often come with undisguised imperfections.

So, I am ready to let go of this flawed dancer, and fall fully in love with the imperfect goddesses who share my own imperfect life. Their bodies, too, are wonders of the world.

108 BELOVED OBJECTS

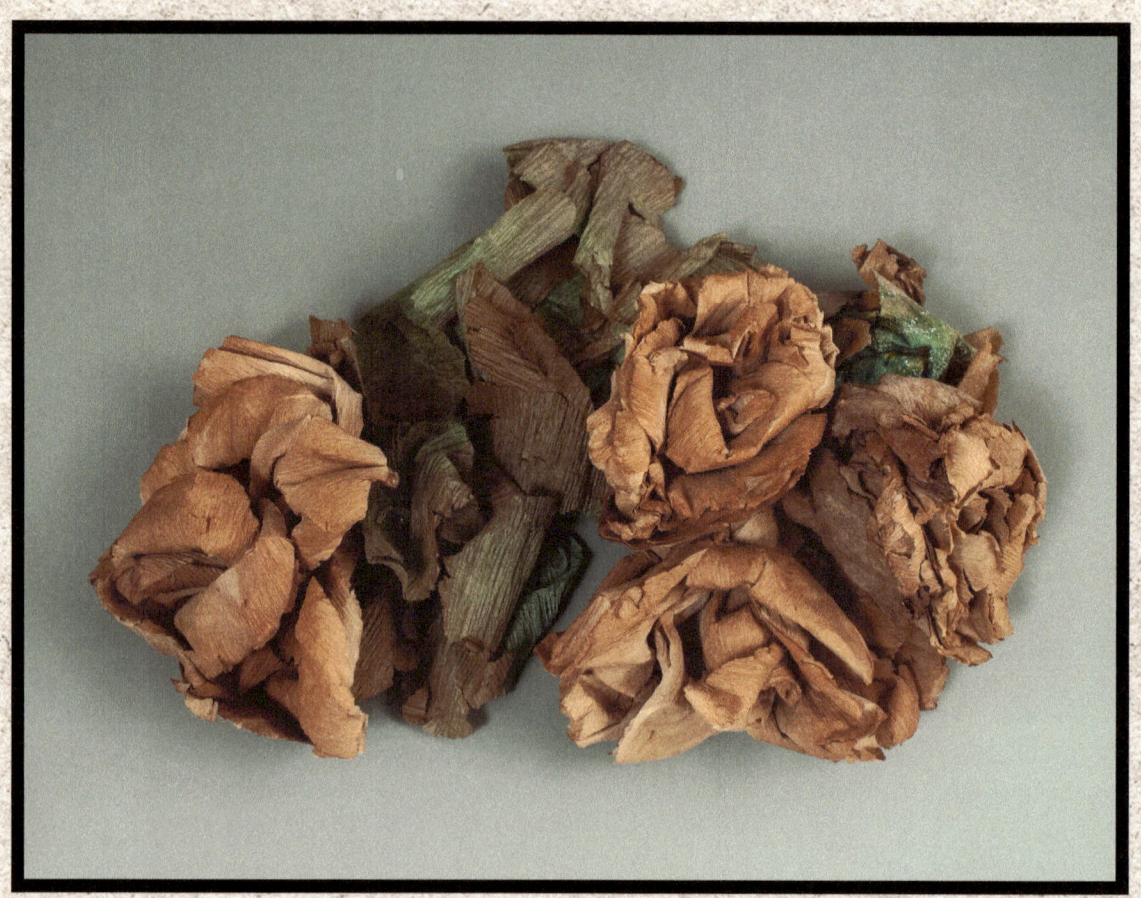

Mexican Paper Roses
OAKLAND, 1988

When I started dating Carina I was nonplussed by her black BMW. It seemed ostentatious for a Latina who worked as a physician's assistant in a homeless shelter. But she glanced at me from behind the wheel, flashing her huge dark eyes. "It's an acronym," she explained. "Beautiful Mexican Woman."

Carina wasn't an artist by profession, but the traditional arts of Mexico fascinated her—especially the memorial *ofrendas* created for *Dia de los Muertos*: Day of the Dead. We shared that obsession. In November 1984, just one month after my father died, I'd been sent to Lake Pátzcuaro by *Islands* magazine to write about the graveside rituals on the island of Janitzio. It was my introduction to that world, and I'd never witnessed anything more beautiful and strange.

We traveled together to Nepal, India, and later Mexico. By that time Carina was apprenticed to a renowned *altarista*, and deeply focused on ritual and assemblage. She turned out to be a gifted artist, skilled at metamorphosis. Her dream was to open a gallery called *Casa Ganesha*, showcasing the best of Mexican and South Asian arts.

At some point during her apprenticeship, Carina made me these flowers. They were mounted on the wall above my stereo for more than 20 years. Fashioned from crepe paper and wire, the petals were originally white.

We lasted until shortly after my brother died, in 1990. Her memory lingered; Carina was the inspiration for characters in two of my books. Neither truly conveys her sweetness or her radiance. Somehow, even after a quarter century, these faded roses do.

108 BELOVED OBJECTS

Guitar Strap
PLAINVIEW, 1970

Paul Kantner—singer, songwriter, and rhythm guitarist for Jefferson Airplane (and, later, Jefferson Starship)—died on January 28th, 2016. He was 75.

As a teenager, I listened to and sang along with their albums incessantly. *After Bathing at Baxter's* and *Crown of Creation* were gospel to me.[2]

But it wasn't really Kantner, or even the vampish Grace Slick, who fascinated me. I was captivated by Jack Casady, the bands' bassist, who later became half of Hot Tuna. For a number of years I noodled with the bass, and was able to fake dumbed-down versions of the traditional standards at which he and guitarist Jorma Kaukonan excelled. In 1971, emboldened by youth, my friend Bob and I started a band called *Clamdaddy*. We played shamelessly at tiny coffee houses as audience members poked each other and wondered, sometimes out loud, what we were doing on the stage—on any stage.

I sold my maple-necked Fender Precision bass when I moved to California in 1974, and that was that. But when Kantner died, I started listening to the Airplane again. Within days I'd bought a used bass on Craigslist and a rumble amp on Amazon. I started taking weekly lessons. This time, by God, I was actually going to learn how to play.

Two years and about 70 lessons later, I know enough to be deeply embarrassed by the musical arrogance of my teens. But I still love the bass, and I'll stick with it—not to emulate the great Jack Casady, but because music is a language worth learning, and the bass is a relatively forgiving place to begin.

My new Squire bass is red, with a thin black leather strap. My original Fender was white, and looked good with this braided strap. Please give it a good home. You can have the name Clamdaddy as well.

---

2   *While working for the weekly Independent in Santa Cruz in 1977, I got to interview Kantner and Grace Slick (they were married at the time) at their gothic mansion on Fulton Street in San Francisco. They got me so stoned I nearly had to be carried out.*

108 BELOVED OBJECTS

Love

A Small Painting
ALMATY, KAZAKHSTAN, 1995

There are places that draw travelers, but there are names as well: Lhasa, Hollywood, Timbuktu. Throughout Central Asia, names that have always beguiled me whisper tales of salt traders, camels, the mysteries of silk: Samarkand, Bukhara, Tashkent.

During my visit to Almaty, I was introduced to a lovely Kazakh woman who worked for a U.S. aid agency as a translator. She took a day off to be my guide. Almaty, she told me, means "Father of Apples"; it is the place where all apples originated. She remarked on how the Soviets—though their architecture was bleak—had planted countless trees in the city: so many trees that one can walk across Almaty and never leave their shade. We visited markets selling mare's yogurt, shared a lamb sandwich under a tree, and mused about her Mongol heritage. By the day's end, we were holding hands. When we parted, she gave me this small painting as a gift.

Travel, for me, is more about people than places. On a side trip to neighboring Uzbekistan, I'd sketched every character in detail: Artur, the droll but perpetually disoriented driver who spirited me from the wild subway stations of Tashkent to sandy Samarkand; old *Dya Dya* ("Uncle") Sinia, navigating the potholed road to Bukhara in his Volga sedan as the white sun baked my knees like potatoes; Philip and Michele, two enterprising Peace Corps volunteers who were bringing internet access to the ancient cities of the Silk Road: the world's first information superhighway.

But I got lazy in Kazakhstan, and didn't keep up my journal. That comes with a cost. Though any guidebook will remind me how to find the Yasawi Mausoleum or Bibi-Khanym Mosque, my dark-haired guide is now lost to time. She was as warm and elegant and tall as the Kalyan Minaret at sunset… but I have forgotten her name.

108 BELOVED OBJECTS

Geologist's Hard-Rock Hammer
GARDEN CITY, NY, 1973

Astronomy and geology: When I was young, the physical sciences captivated me. They still do, and my Audubon *Field Guide to the Night Sky* is well-thumbed. But geology requires more than stargazing. It takes chemistry, and that's where I fell off the bandwagon. I still remember a lot of things about rocks, and about how our planet was (and is being) formed—but I don't take the same pleasure in identifying rocks as I do in teasing out the constellations.

As a teen, though, I did. One of my favorite escapes (once I'd learned to drive) was Garvie's Point, a cliffy, rocky beach on Long Island's north shore. The Point's geology thrilled me. Its narrow beach is strewn with a huge variety of rocks, deposited by the glaciers that retreated at the end of the last Ice Age. *"The boulders emphasize the variety of rocks that were plucked up from geologically diverse areas north of Long Island,"* the website says. *"They were carried along in the ice, as if on a huge conveyor belt, and finally dropped at the base or margin of the glacier."*

My geology professor at Nassau Community College "loaned" me this hammer. I'd bring it to Garvie's Point and crack those boulders open, looking for pink feldspar or rose quartz or iron oxide deposits: those deep red Indian paint pots.

One of my first dates with my first girlfriend, C., was a trip to the Point. It was raining hard. But I put on my goggles, pulled the hammer from my daypack, and began bashing at one of the boulders. C. watched incredulously. "I'll never forget the sight of you kneeling there," she told me years later, "with rain running off your goggles and down your nose, like a man obsessed." What I was *really* obsessed with, I think, was impressing C.

It's far more impressive, I've since learned, to be able to name the constellations on a warm summer night. So this hammer can go—but I'm holding on to my telescope.

108 BELOVED OBJECTS

I Love You Lamp

OAKLAND, 1997

I met Helen in San Francisco, at a reading for *The Size of the World*. She was staring at me, *glowing* at me, from the fourth row of the audience. I had never seen a more beautiful woman. She held a copy of my book—even from my perch on the stage, I could see that it bristled with Post-It notes. My single hope was that she would ask me to sign it.

Helen did approach the signing table, and handed me the book—along with a beautifully wrapped package. "Open it now," she said. Inside was a small, white, wooden horse. It was a deeply personal gift: I'd written about my connection with a certain white horse in my book. I was speechless. Her smile was a mimosa on a Tahitian beach.

Helen came to my house three times a week for the next two months. She'd arrive before dawn, use her key, and crawl into bed with me. Our trysts were brief: She lived with her boyfriend, who left early for the gym. She had to get home before he did.

She was tall, blonde, and curvy, and loved to be spanked—hard. *Really* hard. I was never super comfortable with that. I'm sure my downstairs neighbor wasn't, either.

Was it love? Yes. At least, I pretended it was. But it was more a trajectory. We'd climbed into a catapult, and sprung the catch. We were riding gravity's rainbow.

When I left for Los Angeles to work on my *Star Trek* book, Helen flew down to meet me for a day. We went to Disneyland, seeking out the tiny pockets of untrammeled nature scattered amid the elves and androids. The next morning, as she dressed to go, it seemed something about her had changed. It took me a minute: She was wearing an enormous engagement ring. She smiled sheepishly. "Congratulations," I said.

Our intermezzo ended. She mailed me this lamp about a month later. I've never known what to make of it. It's dopey. The white wooden horse was more convincing.

Helen's engagement flickered, too. I heard she became a doctor, and moved to Alaska. She lives in a tiny town, with few neighbors within earshot.

108 BELOVED OBJECTS

Small Feathered Mask
UNKNOWN (POST-1995)

This object was a gift. I'm not sure which ex-girlfriend it came from, or when. Nor do I know what kind of bird(s) sacrificed those elegant feathers. I'd guess this is the kind of souvenir travelers are discouraged from buying nowadays, when species of every wing, stripe, and scale find themselves on the Endangered list.

I've held onto this, but have never known what to make of it. It is too small to be a real mask for anything but a shrunken head. This means it's purely ornamental. And the expression is unusual. If the face portrayed was not laughing, it would have the stern, threatening look of so many ritual masks. But the countenance is droll: a cheerful, engaging spirit. With a large nose. To tell the truth it looks a bit like my paternal grandmother, Regina Greenwald.

Grandma Regina was already old when I was born; my father had been a Depression-era mistake. She was short and stooped, and suffered from rheumatoid arthritis. Regina was not by any measure a physically attractive woman. But when she was happy—for example, when my brother, sister, and I visited—she'd let loose with a squinty-eyed laugh, like the face on this mask. It set her aglow.

There's certainly a family resemblance. And as with Grandma, so too with me: Smiling, or laughing, improves my appearance a lot.

The more I think about this mask, the more I'm struck by its potential import. Maybe the woman who gave it to me was trying to tell me something about myself; about something I'd misplaced during our time together: a simple joy, expressed without inhibition, when around the people I love.

108 BELOVED OBJECTS

Blue Yo-Yo

OAKLAND, 2000

It was puzzling to receive this yo-yo as one of eight Hanukkah gifts from R., my girlfriend during the end of the millennium.

As a kid I'd tried to learn a few fancy yo-yo tricks and failed. Like every skill that looks easy when an expert does it, mastering Brain Twister, Sleeper, and Rock the Baby proved far beyond the reach of my uncooperative wrist and impatient brain. Things might be different for kids today, when a web search for "best yo-yo tricks" calls up more than a million instructional videos.

When I asked why she'd given me a yo-yo, R. shrugged. Which made me retreat, instantly and unconsciously, into the most comfortable explanation: Sometimes a yo-yo is just a yo-yo.

And sometimes it isn't. It took me about 15 years to figure out that the yo-yo was a metaphor—and a warning—for my level of affection toward R., for my emotional investment in our relationship, for my fluctuating libido, or for all three.

Gaining expertise at anything takes a certain level of commitment, the sweet spot between its objective difficulty and our personal limitations. I never had much of a head for yo-yo tricks. But they seem easy, at least compared to some other skill sets I've abandoned learning, or continue to blunder through. Either way, I've never Rocked the Baby.

108 BELOVED OBJECTS

Salt from the Dead Sea
ISRAEL, 2004

"For reasons that I don't understand, I was born into a species that has an incredibly hard time with itself."

This was the opening line of a talk given today—on Yom Kippur, the Jewish Day of Atonement—by the rabbi of my congregation. He got a good laugh, but it's painfully true. For all our beauty and complexity, he said, despite our capacity for art and love and laughter, humans find being alive a very fraught business.

Though I'm not religious, I observe the "Days of Awe" that fall between Rosh Hashanah (the Jewish New Year) and Yom Kippur. During this eight-day period, it is said, the Book of Life is opened, and our fate for the coming year is decided. "*Who by fire...*" and so on.

The goal of these high holidays is *teshuva*: a homecoming to one's best self. One of the traditional practices is a naming of our shortcomings; the places where we seek a return to wholeness.

On a gorgeous October afternoon, late in the Days of Awe, S. and I spread a picnic blanket on Tennessee Valley Beach. We listed, and then read, our "sins" —including the places where we had fallen short with each other—out loud. It was a pivotal moment. Our bond was fraying, and we were engaged in a fragile task: learning how we could keep loving each other. The sun shimmered on the Pacific, and two curious ravens cocked their heads to watch.

Years ago, for my 50th birthday, I took myself to Israel and floated on the saline surface of the Dead Sea. It's one of the few places on Earth where one can enjoy the sensation of being effortlessly buoyed. As S. and I traded transgressions, I felt a weight lifting from me. The pressure I'd felt on my body and heart for the past month released, and I felt buoyed from below—held in a way that felt natural and warm.

Everything seemed easier after that. Even being myself, with all my failings and weaknesses. It felt like a new starting point. It felt like coming home.

108 BELOVED OBJECTS

Yukata (Japanese Robe)
JAPAN, 1984

We were in many ways polar opposites. Jordan was an aesthete, I a sensualist; he was an academic, I a restless polymath. He was as formal as an Arthurian knight, while I can be crass. He ate no sugar; my own sweet tooth is insatiable. I'm terrible at learning languages—but by the time of his suicide, my brother spoke nearly twenty.

Jordan and I had an admiration for each other that was founded in love, but our day-to-day exchanges were based more on projection than mutual understanding. He once presented me with a gift of Rilke's *Sonnets to Orpheus*, a first edition in German. I spoke not a word. I purchased for him a hardcover edition of *One Hundred Years of Solitude*, which he declined with a snort: "There is no such thing as a translation."

Still, our lives and memories—when they didn't collide—marbled together. Like many strange people, Jordan had an extraordinary memory, and could fill in the missing details of family stories I barely recalled. I trusted that he'd always be there, like a library reference section: a repository of puzzle pieces that made the mural of my life complete.

In the late summer of 1984 I was visiting Japan, staying with my girlfriend Teri. Every evening we would leave our stifling and shower-less apartment and walk the few blocks to the neighborhood *sento*, or public bath. It was permissible to make the trip in one's *yukata*. Mine was simple: a handsome black-and-white cotton print, light and functional. It became so much a part of my experience in Japan that I bought a similar one for Jordan—one of the few souvenir gifts I carried home.

But my homecoming was a strange event, as described elsewhere in this book. I don't recall how long afterwards I gave Jordan this robe. Though I'm sure he accepted it, it lay unwrapped among the artifacts that I found among his possessions.

I was 30 years old in 1984, and 36 when my brother shot himself in his Philadelphia apartment. I'm 67 now. It seems impossible, how time races by. His suicide was 30 years ago. If I live another 33 years, I'll be 100—all but the first few decades of my life passed in a solitude of my own—threaded with unanswerable questions, and unfinished stories.

108 BELOVED OBJECTS

Flower Power

OAKLAND, 2014

I fell in love with a woman who had been sexually abused as a child, and again as an adult. She had a lot of issues. One of her strategies for coping with her trauma was a solo show, which she performed around the San Francisco Bay Area to mixed reviews. The piece had real strengths, but there was a grating undercurrent of fecklessness—the sense that she was an eternal victim, even of those who tried to support her.

Though perpetually broke, she was brilliant, and funny. I've never known anyone like her. She drew the strangest, most surreal comics I've ever seen. One of them featured a tardigrade and an antique violin; another, gleeful talking wildflowers. "I'm afraid to show you my comics," she told me once, "because you'll see how crazy I really am." But I thought they were genius.

She had the most beautiful laugh I've ever heard.

In August of 2014, I bought this grinning, wire-stemmed flower to attach to the handlebars of my bike at Burning Man. I bought a second one for her, because this was the portrait of her in my mind's eye.

For a short time our passions coincided, and we were crazy about each other. Then she fell away. But you know me; I hold onto things. That October, during a run of her show in San Francisco, she told me that a patron was about to give her a $2,000 grant. Could she borrow the money, and pay me back at the end of the week?

Never heard from her again, but we're still Facebook "friends." She's in Hawaii now, a Plumeria in her hair.

108 BELOVED OBJECTS

West Cliff Percussion Ashiko Drum
OAKLAND, 2001

This handsome, well-made drum accompanied me to many New Years' celebrations in Point Reyes, where my friends traditionally rent a house for the holidays. Our hikes, dinners, and drum circles once included R., a beautiful woman I dated from 1999 to 2002. This drum was a gift from her. I'm sad to say we had a rough breakup, filled with anger and convictions of betrayal.

A few months after R. and I parted ways, I visited our neighborhood bookstore for my weekly browse. Now and then I find used copies of my own books, some now out of print. This time—in the travel section—I saw copies of *all* of my books. I pulled one off the shelf. My heart sank as I beheld the loving inscription I'd written to R. years ago, shortly after we'd started dating.

She had traded in every book I'd given her. Who can blame her? I left them on the shelf.

R. got married and moved away. She and her husband lived in France for a spell, and traveled the world before settling in Carmel. In the Spring of 2017, while hiking in the hills above Monterey with a friend, she had a major stroke. The left side of her body was, and remains, almost completely paralyzed.

Though she and I had not communicated for years, a few mutual friends served as intermediaries. With R.'s permission, I was put on the list for updates about her condition. Though they tried to sound upbeat, the prognosis was grim. For someone as active and adventurous as R., the stroke was like being tossed, without cause or warning, into a prison.

R. and I reconciled. More than that; it's fair to say that, with our respective physical challenges, we've bonded. I've visited her in the hospital. Our meetings leave me filled with admiration. As she struggles to regain mobility, R. is navigating her personal nightmare with more grit, courage, and humor than I could ever muster.

I don't play the ashiko anymore. But while I was recovering from my back surgeries, my sister visited. Debra saw the drum, and told me that her husband would love it. A few weeks later, I shipped it to them.

So this particular object is already spoken for. Why include it here? Because I want to share R.'s story. Sometimes we get to choose what we give away. But often, and ultimately, we do not.

108 BELOVED OBJECTS

Sandalwood Ganesha
OAKLAND (VIA INDIA), 1984 & 1996

Ages ago, the great Hindu scribe Valmiki, in a spell of divine inspiration, was composing the great epic *Ramayana*. His pen raged so rapidly across the page that it burst into flame. Ganesh, patron of writers, witnessed the conflagration. To keep Valmiki's momentum from faltering, Ganesh snapped off his right tusk and tossed it to the scribe as a quill. Valmiki powered on, and the *Ramayana* was completed.

During my first visit to Nepal in 1979, I frequented a small temple in Patan. The modest brick structure housed an ancient stone Ganesha, his trunk worn smooth from centuries of caresses, his forehead painted with colorful devotional powder. I fell under the spell of Ganesha, and joined the locals ringing the tangled clusters of bells hanging above the elephant god's head.

When I returned to Nepal in 1984, I took a room in the Chhetrapati Guest House and unloaded my "portable" Smith-Corona, the best manual writing machine of the era. Day after day I drummed on the keys, until one cold, cloudless morning when I found myself staring at a blank page. My hands hovered uselessly over the letters, my thoughts frozen.

At that moment I heard the faint and mournful strains of a blues harp, coming from somewhere in the guest house. The distraction dissolved my writer's block. My fingers fell back into the groove, typing to the music. A page or two later, I left my sunlit deck to find the piper. The hallway was dim, and the unmistakable aroma of hashish emerged from the stairwell. A man with dusty blonde hair sat on a step. Next to him was a smoldering pipe, carved from bone. He lifted it in invitation.

The bluesman, whose spontaneous recital had rebooted the rhythm of my typewriter keys, was another young American traveler named Steve. Like me, he wasn't just passing through. Steve had a fellowship to study Ayurveda from the Nepali masters. We spoke for hours, sharing our enchantment with life in Kathmandu.

Those first magical visits to Nepal are far behind me, but this carved sandalwood Ganesha—a gift from Steve—left a tusk in that world. It still evokes a chaotic cacophony of apple sellers and temple bells, lowing cows and rickshaw *wallahs*, drifting clouds of incense and hashish: a magical time and place in my life when every sense was heightened, all encounters were holy, and the friendships forged would last a lifetime.

108 BELOVED OBJECTS

Unicorn Clock

OAKLAND, 2016

It's a funny thing about nicknames. They're invented to seal a close connection. But I've also watched them fade out of use as a relationship changes, and entrancement evaporates.

For a couple of years, I was her Unicorn. Our dates and texts were filled with unicorn references. Gifts, too: unicorn Band-Aids, unicorn socks, Unicorn Gold toilet freshener. A unicorn onesie to wear on our weekend trip to Safari West. And this Lucite unicorn clock, which she found in an antique shop window. I can imagine her glee: It's so cool to know you've found the perfect Christmas present.

Now it's Christmas again, three years later. We walked around Lake Merritt yesterday, a three-mile loop, and never once held hands.

These days she calls me *Jefe*. We're sort of like family now. Though I don't feel like the boss of anyone, I'm glad I still have a nickname—but there's nothing magical about it.

The unicorn clock never made it to the bedroom wall. It balances unsteadily on my dresser, just behind the unicorn piggy bank.

I was her Unicorn—and she was my Jungle Cat. She always will be. But time has tamed our bond. The claws and fur have been trimmed, and her nickname condensed to "JC."

108 BELOVED OBJECTS

Wishing Lamp
ORINDA, CA, 2017

My friend David is the smartest person I know. He's an artist, an inventor, an engineer, a jeweler, a filmmaker, and a student of history with almost total recall. He's even been on *Jeopardy!*—though he lost when he forgot to phrase his answer as a question. Heartbreaking!

We met in Santa Barbara in 1980, part of a thriving local art scene. The action centered around a few fearless galleries and the newly minted Summer Solstice Celebration. We were full of creative energy, big ideas, long-term ambitions, visions of immortality. David was already on his way to fame; he'd painted a mural at UC Santa Barbara, a visual journey through Rodrigo's *Concierto de Aranjuez*. Visitors could listen to the music and follow its movement in the painting. Cerebral, perhaps, but beautiful.

In 1989, David invented the world's first omnidirectional video camera: a soccer ball-sized marvel able to film in all directions at once. He used it to shoot the first fully immersive color movie, set at a staged basketball game. David now holds some 50 patents, most recently for a hand-powered water purification system.

We were close for many years, and communicated daily. But after David and his wife moved to Oregon, and I to Oakland, we fell out of touch. After a long hiatus, I learned that he'd had a showdown with thyroid cancer. He beat it, thank God.

David's only sibling, an older brother who lived in the Bay Area, died in 2017. When David came down to clear out his brother's home, we had a brief reunion. I stood around uselessly, watching him sort through books, antiques, photographs, knick-knacks. When he unearthed this wishing lamp charm, he gave it to me as a gift.

I asked him for his three wishes first. "I'd beg for the U.S. not to get into a war," he said. "Next, that we will be wise enough to know how to deal with the things that threaten us—whether AI, revivified fossil diseases, or climate change. Wish number three: that what I've contributed to the world, through my patents and art, will be appreciated."

I appreciate you David, even though I'm giving this lamp away. One of my three wishes? That you get a second chance on *Jeopardy!*.

108 BELOVED OBJECTS

Souvenir Moai

RAPA NUI (EASTER ISLAND), 2006

The Southern Hemisphere's Timbuktu is an isolated landfall 2,290 miles off the coast of Chile. The closer you get, the faster its name changes—like one of the elusive destinations in Italo Calvino's *Invisible Cities*.

What I knew as Easter Island (a Portuguese explorer first visited on Easter, 1722) became *Isla de Pasqua* on my boarding pass from Santiago. On landing I learned I was actually on *Rapa Nui*: The Big Island. And moving deeper into the landscape, across grassy hills punctuated by fallen and restored *moai*, I heard a quieter name: *Te Pito O Te Henua*, The Navel of the World.

There are 887 huge *moai* in all. Legend claims some literally walked to their final locations using their *mana*: spiritual power. Though they look stern, they were not meant to threaten. These were protector deities. Erected in rows along the rocky coastline, they face not the ocean but inland, watching over their tribes.

Their purpose, dates of creation, and means of transport are vague. History, on Rapa Nui, is a pliant commodity. Stories are passed within families, between families, to archeologists and journalists, guidebook authors, and crackpots. No one knows anything for sure. This is not a problem. To the contrary; it's as if many universes are possible.

The leader of my press trip to Rapa Nui was a tall German woman. We'd traveled together before, and I was hopelessly in love with her. I wanted nothing more than to be her *moai*; to watch over her through the centuries, keeping all dangers at bay. We spent many hours together on the island. One day, tired of shopping for souvenirs, we visited the post office. The clerk agreed to stamp our passports with Easter Island postmarks. Those, my journals, and this—the *moai* she helped me choose—are all I'll ever need to recall the mysteries, and my unrequited dreams, on Rapa Nui.

At a certain point in our lives, the *moai* within us start to pivot, turning from the tempest and toward the slower-moving rhythms of our inner landscape. It's all right. I'm not there yet, but the *mana* is rising. Because no matter which way I face, nothing is fully lost. I can still hear the waves, the *thwop* of rubber stamps on paper, the musical laughter rising from the possible worlds I might have inhabited.

Meditation Bowl

SPIRIT ROCK, 2007

I first met Tenzin Gyatso, the 14th Dalai Lama of Tibet, in early July of 1979.

    At the time I was traveling through India, at the tail end of an epic bout with dysentery. I had arrived in McCleod Ganj, a Tibetan refuge on a hill above the Dharamshala valley. Drinking *po-cha* at a small restaurant, I ran into a friend we'd met in Kathmandu: a Mexican journalist named Anna Victoria.

Anna was ecstatic: She had just received permission to interview His Holiness for a Mexican magazine. When I asked if she needed a photographer, her eyes lit up. "*Claro!*" she exclaimed.

My recollection of that morning is dim, but I was sure I'd made a fool of myself. So I searched through a plastic bin in my closet to find the journal I'd kept in 1979. The entry from that day—predictably titled "Hello, Dalai"—contradicted my uncharitable memory. In fact, I had felt blessed by the opportunity to meet the man—though at the age of 25, I had little concept of who the Dalai Lama was.

The "simple Tibetan monk" greeted us with genuine pleasure, curious eyes, and a disarming lack of formality. While Anna asked questions, I fiddled with my flash and settings, trying to get a good shot despite glaring backlight. *He regarded me with definite interest*, I'd written afterwards. *My regret was not being able to return his gaze, except through the meticulously focused lens of the camera.*

A few years later, the Dalai Lama visited Santa Barbara to give a public talk. I'd moved there in 1980, and by then had some Buddhist education. My friends and I were seated in the third row of the auditorium when His Holiness walked onto the stage. The house lights were up, and he scanned the audience. Immediately his eyes caught mine. He smiled. I looked from side to side, certain he meant someone else—but the Dalai Lama pointed at me emphatically. He then pantomimed a camera, peering intensely through a phantom viewfinder as his finger snapped an invisible shutter. My mouth dropped open; he pointed at me again, and laughed.

Years later, the Spirit Rock Meditation Center invited me to tell a story about the Dalai Lama. That story, though very different, also paid homage to his remarkable memory. Having lit many candles in Tibetan temples, I think now of some lines by the Greek poet George Seferis:

> *What can a flame remember? If it remembers a little less than is necessary, it goes out. If it remembers a little more than is necessary, it goes out. If only it could teach us, while it burns, to remember correctly.*

The gift I received for my Spirit Rock story was this beautiful meditation bowl. I'm gifting it to my goddaughter Amy, a wise soul. I hope she'll remember me correctly—or, at least, charitably.

108 BELOVED OBJECTS

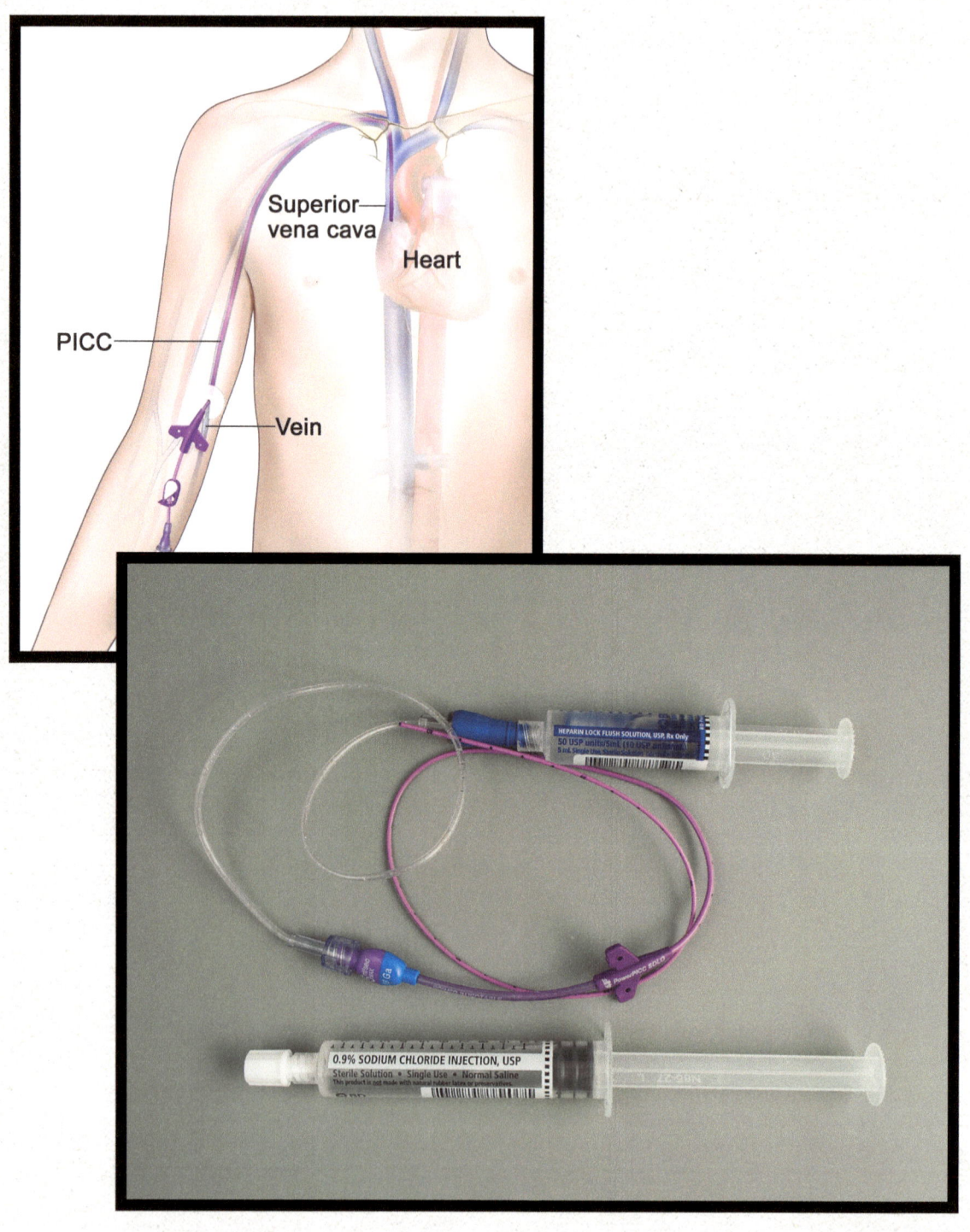

PICC (Peripherally Inserted Central Catheter) Line

OAKLAND, 2018

How often can you hold in your hands something that was literally inside your heart?

This PICC line was fed through a vein in my right arm, and wiggled up the blood vessel into my own heart's right atrium. For six weeks, once every eight hours, I used the port end of the PICC line to "push" a powerful antibiotic into my body.

All of this began with a routine spinal epidural I received in mid-February 2018, with the hopeful goal of alleviating the persistent discomfort in my lower back and left leg. But the epidural, unbeknownst to me, seeded a staph injection in my lumbar spine. That spring, as I traveled to Nepal and Thailand, the infection spread. It consumed one of my discs, ate away at my vertebrae, and poisoned my bloodstream.

I had imagined—during the months of pain, night sweats, and fevers—that the issue was mechanical: My chronic back problem was getting worse. My doctor wasn't so sure. So after returning home, I had my blood tested. When the rheumatologist saw the results, he ordered me to the ER. I spent a week in the hospital, touch and go, before being sent home with this PICC line in my arm. It was removed two months later.

I'd never been seriously ill before, not in a life-threatening way. I'd never even spent a night in the hospital. This scary affirmation of my mortality was a deeply humbling event, which I hope I met with grace and some humor.

Among its other gifts, the crisis also served as a proof-of-concept for me. All my life, I've worked to build and cultivate friendships, and to show up for the many people I care about. I guess that on some level I was building a foundation: a community of interrelated friends who would, if needed, show up for me.

"If" became "when." And they did. Nothing in my experience prepared me for the level of support I received from family and friends. Their generosity reached deeper than any PICC line, and will remain in my heart forever. I don't need this macabre souvenir as a reminder.

Endings

A few days after my brother died, I visited his Philadelphia apartment. The shock of his suicide was still fresh. It was breathtakingly strange to walk through the four rooms—bedroom, living room, bathroom, kitchen—with the awareness that I'd never see him again.

Jordan had led a Spartan life. He didn't have many possessions, outside the essentials: clothing, razor, comb, pots and pans, lamps, notepads and pencils. And his journals, of course. But I hoped to find a keepsake: an object I could carry on my person. A talisman; something that would keep Jordan close to me in the decades to come.

In the single drawer of his bedroom night table, I found two candidates: a simple pocket watch (which has its own chapter), and a Swiss Army Knife.

The knife became my constant companion. Though I wasn't sure how much use Jordan had gotten from it—the blades were unblemished and factory-sharp—the knife was a reminder of my brother's efficiency, his conviction that one should never say or do anything more than necessary.

Three years later, while trekking in Nepal's Annapurna Sanctuary, I stopped for lunch at a tea shop in Tatopani. There was a long wooden table outside; a good place to grab a bite and catch up in my journal. As my momos were being served, a small trekking group limped into view. There were five Western hikers, and three local porters. One of the porters was being helped along, almost hanging between two of the trekkers. He was delirious with pain, his head waggling loosely.

"We need help," one of the men called out. "We need to lay this man down." I stood up and moved away from the table. They lowered the porter onto the wooden slats. "I'm a doctor," the trekker said hoarsely. "This man has a dangerous abscess in his abdomen. If I can't drain it, he'll likely die."

I saw the lump under the porter's skin, the size of half a tennis ball. "How can I help?"

"I need some boiling water," the doctor said, "And a sharp steel knife." He looked at the porter and grimaced. "And some strong *rakshi*, if you have it," he added. "I'm packing suture thread and needles, but no anesthetic."

The *sowni* managing the tea shop hurried inside to fulfill his requests. A pot of steaming water was set on a bench; one of the porter's companions drizzled the strong local liquor into his friend's mouth. The knives on offer were razor sharp, but huge; more like machetes than surgical tools. "These won't work," the doctor said. He turned to me. "Have you got a pocketknife?"

I did. It was in my right front pocket, leashed to a belt loop with a green cord. The doctor opened it up, and nodded. "This will do."

* * *

I won't convey the play-by-play of that surgery, but—for the short run, at least—it was successful. The porter's life was saved. My brother's knife, of course, was covered with pus and blood. The doctor dropped it into the pot with the still-hot water. "Take this inside," he instructed the *sowni*, "and boil it for ten minutes."

That is what she did. But when the knife was returned to me, it wasn't the same. The red plastic cover had warped and melted, exposing the steel casement beneath.

"You ruined my knife!" I cried, reflexively. The doctor gave me a hard look.

It took weeks for me to accept that the poached relic of that medical emergency—usable, but unrecognizable—was still Jordan's knife. Until the surgery, it was as if he'd been on the trek with me. And years later, when I actually *did* lose the knife in the High Sierra, it felt like I'd lost my brother all over again. Eventually I bought a new one—and managed to convince myself that it was a reincarnation of the original, which had "died" at my campsite in Yosemite.

So it is with objects. Sometimes they take us back to the beginning of things; sometimes they're what we're left with at the end. But the objects themselves, as always, have nothing to say. They are priceless or worthless, depending on the stories we tell ourselves.

108 BELOVED OBJECTS

Endings

Burl Pipe

PLAINVIEW, NEW YORK, 1971

What's more pretentious than a 17-year-old smoking a pipe?

My favorite blend was The Balkan Sobranie, "a traditional mixture of rich Virginia, Latakia and rare Yenidje tobaccos." It came in a classy round tin, as pictured.

But the pipe thing… what was I up to? Who was I emulating? Cary Grant? Hemingway? Gandalf? My life as an adolescent is a mystery to me. I know that I was a fearful kid, sometimes bullied (it's hard to avoid bullying a pipe-smoking teenager), and that I often sought refuge in books. Lacking good parental role models, I latched onto literary figures from the past. Mark Twain fascinated me, as did Dr. Seuss. And Sherlock Holmes, of course, smoked a pipe.

But maybe it wasn't the pipe at all. Maybe it was the tobacco, with its exotic notes of the Middle East and Turkey: pipe dreams to my teenage mind, seeding the ground for a life of wanderlust.

Later that year, I discovered a different kind of pipe. I soon gave up tobacco—and got my first passport.

108 BELOVED OBJECTS

King Birendra Whiskey Decanter
THAMI, NEPAL, MID-1990S

Sometimes I think we need a king. Not just the U.S., but the world. And not a traditional king, but a brilliant, wise, and benevolent ruler: someone who will decree universal health care, command that carbon emissions be brought down to survivable levels, and transform our economy into the engine of a green, humanistic utopia. Like King Arthur, but vegan and tech-savvy.

Birendra was not such a monarch. He was a disinterested and ineffectual king who preferred to stay at home, smoke cigars, and watch Bruce Lee movies. But he was benign—so benign that he was allowed to keep his head, and stay on as a constitutional monarch, after being overthrown during Nepal's 1990 "People Power" revolution.

After the revolution Birendra was rebranded, by the Nepalis, from a despised despot into a beloved figurehead. He was the glue that held the nation together. Beneath the centuries-old symbol of his royal scepter, the nearly 100 ethnic groups living within Nepal's landlocked borders—from the Tharu of the hot, flat lowlands to the Sherpa in the breathless Himalaya—found their common denominator. Birendra, and his notion of a "Zone of Peace," became central to Nepal's identity.

When King Birendra and nine members of his family were gunned down during the Royal Palace Massacre in 2001, that connective tissue disintegrated. After a period of disbelief and despair, Nepal was cast adrift, and forced to find a new coherence. Two decades have passed since Birendra was assassinated but, even now, many Nepali citizens would be unable to define what binds their republic together (aside from the dread of being absorbed by neighboring China and/or India).

A therapist once asked me what kept me together, what kept me going. "I live to travel, and to hike," I told her. But ever since my body has been compromised—initially by a staph infection, then by two subsequent spinal surgeries—I have descended into an existential crisis. Everything I was revolved around my love of the outdoors, the exhilaration of travel, and sharing those vocations with friends and lovers. With my ability to do either in jeopardy, I no longer know who I am, or how to explain myself to myself. My very identity seems to be fading. Like Nepal in 2001, I am suffused with disbelief and, often, despair.

Will my ability to do what I love return, given time? Is patience all I need? These are unknowns. In the meantime, what I need is a drink. (This really is a decanter, by the way, fabricated upon an empty bottle of Johnnie Walker Red. The head comes off.)

108 BELOVED OBJECTS

Brass Temple Bells
SANTA CRUZ, 1977-1982

During the summer of 1977, after getting my BA in psychology, I took a temp job with Pacific Bell. I was trained to make basic repairs and, when needed, convert those old four-wire telephone lines to the new, plug-and-play phone outlets. Every morning I'd pick up a stack of work orders at the office, and drive my PacBell van all over Santa Cruz County. Grass, cocaine, sex... there was nothing people wouldn't give for a new Princess phone, or an extra jack in their bathroom.

During my first days on the job I finished my assignments early, and hurried back to the dispatch desk for more. On Thursday, one of the repairmen took me aside. "We don't get paid extra for doing twice the work," the old-timer told me, "You're just making the rest of us look bad." Later that day, I followed him to the glade and swimming hole where he and the other drivers hid their vans once they'd finished their quota.

Sometimes I joined my fellow workers for an afternoon smoke and swim. But often I'd drive home, and spend the afternoon hours building sculptures. These were offbeat assemblages of wood and leather, brass fittings, random pieces of fur, found objects, textiles, and small bells. All were meant to be touched, played with, manipulated. Inspired by Alexander Calder, whose mobiles enchanted me, I thought of my works as abstract "busy boxes"—crib toys for adults.

My career as an artist was short-lived, though I did achieve a bit of success as a graphic designer. Ultimately it made more sense to turn my energy toward writing, which has always been a passion. The appeal of visual art, I realized, can be purely subjective—but everyone loves a good story.

But I missed doing sculpture. Twenty years later, by then a full-time writer living in Oakland, I had an idea: I'd rent a studio, and start making art again. A no-frills workspace on Adeline Street came up on Craigslist, and I pounced. For decades, I'd been schlepping my art supplies—including this string of bells—from place to place. At last they had a home. Who knew what I might create?

It didn't take. As the months passed I visited my studio maybe once a week, producing virtually nothing. Sad, but true. The muses that once inspired me had fled—or changed direction. So... No more busy boxes for me. Just stories. I ring the bells that still can ring.

108 BELOVED OBJECTS

Kodak Beaker

PLAINVIEW, NY, 1984

The last time I saw my father was in early 1983. He was driving me to New York's JFK to catch a flight overseas. I was off on a year-long Rotary Journalism Fellowship to Nepal. My mom sat restlessly in the passenger seat. We'd warned my father not to take the Chrysler—Mom's Ford was more reliable—but his personal anthem was the Frank Sinatra song "My Way," and as always, he had ignored our advice. I sat in the back seat, listening to them quarrel, the familiar soundtrack of my life at home.

The Chrysler broke down, as predicted. We were already running late. While my father tried in vain to restart the engine, I exited the car in disgust, pulled my backpack from the trunk, and stuck out my thumb.

During my 18 months abroad, I asked friends returning home to carry parcels of my exposed Kodachrome film. Reluctantly, I decided to rely on my father to process the film, review the slides, and write to tell me if my exposures were okay. At first, his notes were perfunctory. As the months went by, though, he wrote increasingly perceptive letters about my images: praising the beauty of Nepal, the clarity of light, the vivid festivals. He began to ask me for advice about how to get started in photography. Within a year he had bought a good camera, and set up a small darkroom in our basement laundry room.

Near the end of my trip, I phoned home from a three-day stopover in Hong Kong. My Dad had all the lenses he needed, but asked me to find him a pair of fine binoculars. "I trust your judgment," he said. It was the first time he'd ever expressed confidence in me.

A few days later I landed at LAX. Jet-lagged and culture-shocked, I called home again. My brother—who should have been away at college—answered the phone. "Jord!" I said. "What are you doing home?"

"Dad is dead," he announced. "He died of a massive heart attack last night."

I was on a cross-country flight within hours, and home the next morning: sitting *shiva*, going through my father's effects, and standing in his darkroom, bereft. I would never meet the man who, after 30 years of disinterest, had at last become a friend.

108 BELOVED OBJECTS

Butter Lamp Wicks
NEPAL, 1989

Tijar, the autumn Festival of Lights, is one of the most beautiful celebrations in Nepal. The holiday honors Laxmi, the Hindu goddess of wealth, whose *vahana* (vehicle) is an owl. Gold coins rain from her palms. On the night of her celebration, simple mandalas called *rangoli*—created with colored powder and marigold petals—are drawn like spirit catchers on the paths leading into private homes and businesses. Butter lamps glow in windows and doorways, meant to attract the generous goddess.

Or so it was, long ago. These days, garish Christmas lights, mass produced in China or India, are draped like curtains over homes and storefronts. Cascades of bright bulbs blanket the entrances of banks and supermarkets, filling the narrow streets of Kathmandu with a manic blaze.

On the night of Laxmi Puja, in November of 1989, I wandered into Asan Tole and Indrachowk, two of the oldest neighborhoods in Kathmandu. The streets were packed. There was a wild, party atmosphere. Powerful firecrackers exploded, dogs ran off in terror, and a million electric lights blinked epileptically above the revelers.

Suddenly, there was a different kind of explosion: A vintage generator, atop a nearby metal pole, shorted out with a shower of blue and red sparks. The streets were plunged into darkness. Everything came to a halt, and a thousand people caught their breath. All one could see, in every direction, were the flames of flickering butter lamps, burning by the doorways and on the window sills of the poorest, most traditional homes.

It was as if a spell had been cast. The lovely *rangoli* along the street sides—until now ignored, or carelessly trampled—glowed with the light of candles within. There was giggling, whispers, and near-total silence. Even the dogs ventured back to the streets.

And then, without warning, power was restored. The streets and squares were again at the mercy of flashing lights, pulsing Bollywood soundtracks, the sizzle of cherry bomb fuses. But in that last instant—the immeasurable moment after electricity returned but before the melee resumed—I heard a collective sigh of sadness.

These cotton butter lamp wicks were purchased a few minutes later, for about a dime, at a tiny street stall selling lentils, rice, and chilies. They seemed both magical and sad: like the fuses of a broken time machine.

108 BELOVED OBJECTS

Endings

Painted Souvenir Wooden Shoe
HOLLAND, 1971

My first solo trip abroad was a disaster.

I was just out of high school and eager to get away from my combative home in Plainview, New York. A youthful obsession with solo travel had grown out of two films—*Lawrence of Arabia* and *2001: A Space Odyssey*—as well as a photography book called *Navajo Wildlands* by Elliot Porter. The world was beckoning.

My plan was to spend the whole summer—10 weeks—exploring Europe. But at 17, emerging from a confidence-shattering family life, I was too weak to survive as a stranger in a strange land. Shortly after arriving in Copenhagen on a $99 excursion fare, a pall of anxiety and depression fell upon me. I became inexplicably, desperately homesick. Though my humiliation was acute, it was an overpowering condition. No amount of scrawling in my spiral-bound journal—which I filled with self-flagellating prose and religious claptrap (I was observant at the time)—did anything to calm my mind.

Motion seemed to help. Desperate to relieve my angst, I wore out my Eurail Pass, racing from Denmark to Germany to Italy, through France and Belgium, snapping picture after picture with my Kodak Instamatic 104, as if a visual record of my checklist tour would absolve me of my failure as a solo traveler. Photos were not always enough; buying souvenirs was necessary as well. An Omega watch in Geneva; Belgian chocolates; a small but weighty replica of Michelangelo's *Moses* in Rome; a wooden Dutch shoe.

Nothing worked. After a few weeks, I flew back home in disgrace.

Soon after, I discovered an easier (and cheaper) escape route. One night, after partying with some friends, I painted the Dutch shoe gaily. It was instantly transformed. No longer a reminder of my hobbled journey, it became an accessory on my new journeys: a psychedelic ashtray, holding the smoldering joints that, for a few years, replaced one kind of trip with another.

108 BELOVED OBJECTS

Chess Pawn (Hydrocal™ & Resin)
SAN FRANCISCO, 1986

During my first visit to Kathmandu, an artist named Michael Pedroni had an opening at the American Cultural Center. His work was vivid and surreal, often tricking the eye. One painting portrayed a group of Buddhist monks. Few people noticed that one of the monks, clad in a red and yellow robe, was missing his head.

There was a guest book, and I filled a page with commentary; a virtual review, as Michael later recalled, of which paintings I liked, which I didn't, and why. Pretty obnoxious. But my hubris won his attention, and we became friends—first in Nepal, then after we'd returned to the Bay Area.

Michael lived with his wife, Patrice, in a North Beach fourplex. The building had been in his family since 1944. In the basement was his office, which also served as a small library and gallery. On the desk sat a chess set that Michael had made in 1970. The pawns were fists—a nice metaphorical touch. I'll never forget the moment when Michael, grinning broadly, instructed me to push on one of the bookshelves. The office wall swung away, opening onto a large studio filled with works-in-progress, crazy sculptures, and vintage props from Playland-by-the-Sea.

In 1986, Michael and Patrice rented the flat above them to a Latina medical worker named Carina. I met her right after she moved in. Carina laughed that she hadn't even bought herself a toothbrush yet; I mailed her one the next day. We became lovers soon after, and traveled together to Mexico, India, and Nepal.

On March 10th, 1990, the four of us—along with Michael and Patrice's two young daughters—celebrated my birthday in the Pedroni's kitchen. The evening was a blur; I'd returned four days earlier from another long trip to Asia. Carina was pouring red wine when her upstairs phone began to ring. She dashed off to answer it, and returned with a puzzled expression. "It's your mother," Carina told me. "She sounds… awful."

"I'll be right back," I said. But the person who left that party never came back.

108 BELOVED OBJECTS

Pocket Watch

PHILADELPHIA, 1990

This was my brother Jordan's pocket watch. I found it among the scant possessions left in his Philadelphia apartment, a few days after he took his life. Books; toiletries; a pocket knife; this watch.

This is not an heirloom. It's a Pulsar, battery-run, worth $150 or so (if it were working; a few years ago the watch stopped, and a new battery didn't fix it). It's unlikely Jordan bought this for himself. He very rarely bought anything for himself. My guess is that it was a gift from a friend. My brother had many affectations, but it's hard to imagine him succumbing to a pocket watch.

I did, though. I carried this watch for many years. It fit neatly into the small pocket in my jeans—a pocket designed, in the 19th century, for just such a purpose.

Jordan killed himself on the morning of March 9th, 1990. A woman who lived a few apartments down the hall told me that, as she was leaving for work, she saw him standing despondently in his doorway. She hugged me, and sobbed. "If only I'd spoken to him," she said. "If only I'd given him a hug."

Every member of my family has suffered from depression, to varying degrees. Father, mother, sister, brother. Today especially, I feel the weight of those demons alighting on my own chest, making my breath shallow. And while I have enough to be genuinely depressed about, this latest series of spells feels like something else. It comes on like a quick-acting drug, always in the early morning, filling my body with a tsunami of despair so powerful that it washes me far inland. Another wave might carry me back; it may not. You can never be sure.

I don't know what time it was when Jordan last looked at this watch. But I do know the last words he wrote in his journal, on March 8th, 1990: *I cannot bear to wake another day to sorrow.*

I hear you, my brother. I understand why you let go of everything, and left us all for a place beyond time.

108 BELOVED OBJECTS

Endings

Portable Game Board

MADRAS, INDIA, FEBRUARY 1990

I purchased this fold-up game at a train station in Madras. It opens into two playing boards. On one side there's Ludo, a version of the Indian game Pachisi. On the other is Snakes & Ladders, a game that may be close to 2,000 years old. In 1943 it was imported to America, rebranded as "Chutes & Ladders" for the snake-loathing Christian nation.

I don't recall how often Carina and I played these games on the Howrah Express; we had many rattling hours of leisure. What I do remember is the gnawing impatience of vacationing in India while a long-overdue revolution gathered steam in Nepal. And having to explain to Carina that, even though we might never again visit the sultry southern beaches of Tamil Nadu, my place at that moment was in Kathmandu: recording the overthrow of Nepal's monarchy for the *San Francisco Examiner*.

I had no idea at the time, but my three closest relationships would be transformed that season. Nepal—for centuries "The World's Only Hindu Kingdom"—became a clumsy and corrupt republic. And when Carina and I reunited in San Francisco, our already fragile bond was shattered by a third upheaval: my brother Jordan's suicide.

When I played board games as a kid I took them at face value. One, two, three, ladder; 24, 25, 26, snake. Now, of course, I realize that games are often metaphors for our lives: exhilarating climbs, precipitous descents, picking up the pieces, pushing onward again.

It's sort of unfair. Because while any upward movement demands diligence (ladders don't build themselves), our falls from grace can result from a single misstep. We can also be pushed, without warning, onto an entirely new playing board—and into a game with completely different rules.

Maybe I fucked up that February. Maybe if I'd played a bit differently, I'd have won a Pulitzer for my coverage of Nepal's revolution. Maybe Carina and I would have had kids; my brother, if I could have saved him, would be their uncle.

I know it's a cliché, but honestly? I wish there had been a practice round.

108 BELOVED OBJECTS

Civil Air Patrol Collar Insignia

PLAINVIEW, NY, 1967

There was a time in my life when I wanted desperately to wear a uniform. I took it to some length. At age 16 I wrote my local congressman for a letter of recommendation: a requirement for my application to the Air Force Academy in Colorado.

My motive was simple: I wanted to go to outer space. The logical first step was becoming, like all of the Mercury and Gemini astronauts, a jet pilot.

I've always been fascinated with flying. At 13, I joined the Civil Air Patrol: a civilian wing of the Air Force that flies volunteer search and emergency missions. As a crisp cadet I studied aviation, aerospace, and leadership, reaching the rank of Airman First Class. And I flew, nearly every weekend, in a single-engine Cessna with a very laid-back pilot who taught me the basics of solo flight. I was tempted to get my pilot's license—but it would have cost around $1,500, an unthinkable sum.

So what happened? Puberty, for one thing. Vietnam and the draft. Woodstock, Jefferson Airplane, Kent State, Country Joe, Kurt Vonnegut Jr., and my best friend's bong.

Do I regret abandoning my space-bound aspirations? Yes, actually. By the time I'd grown up, astronauts didn't have to be test pilots or members of the military. These days there may even be stoner astronauts, although they sure don't talk about it.

If I win a billion dollars, or meet a genie, I'll arrange a trip to the International Space Station. And I'll double down for a spacewalk. The very thought of it still leaves me breathless.

Meanwhile, I'll have to be satisfied flying within the Earth's atmosphere: far below the canopy of stars, but wearing what I please.

108 BELOVED OBJECTS

Endings

Shangrila (Royal Nepal Airlines) Tray
NEPAL, 1984

There were two occasions in my life when I thought I would die in an airplane.

The first time, I was a senior at Plainview-Old Bethpage High School on Long Island. My friend Richard, also 17, had just earned his pilot's license. He offered to fly one of our classmates up to Brown University in Providence—a distance of about 150 miles—for an admissions interview, and invited me along for the ride.

All went well at first. But when our single-engine Piper crossed the forests between Connecticut and Rhode Island, we found ourselves engulfed in fog. We were flying blind—and Richard did not have an instrument rating. Even skilled pilots have perished in thick fog. Richard was wide-eyed, suppressing panic, but I managed to inscribe a few last words in my journal. "I have no regrets" I wrote, signing my name with a flourish.

The second time was in April 1984, on a Royal Nepal Airlines flight from Kathmandu to Tumlingtar. I was the only Westerner aboard the twin-engine Otter. Again: sudden, thick fog. This time, though, we were locked in a narrow valley between towering mountains, tossed by turbulence. At any second, a sheer cliff might have materialized in front of us. The pilots were whispering in urgent tones as the passengers—all Sherpas—worked their *mala* beads and chanted Buddhist prayers, preparing for the *bardo*.

I wasn't blasé enough to write my epitaph, but I did recall the opening scenes of Frank Capra's *Lost Horizon*, when Conway's airplane crash-lands in the Himalaya. It had never occurred to me that the "Shangrila" service offered by Royal Nepal Airlines might be an actual promise of that fabled destination.

But we had a kind of insurance. The previous October, I had watched in horror as scores of goats and chickens were led into Kathmandu's airport and sacrificed to the wrathful goddess Kali: their severed heads and blood bestowing divine protection upon the parked aircraft. That grisly ounce of prevention worked—and a shot at stumbling into the enchanted valley of Shangrila, hidden among the snowy peaks, was denied me.

No regrets about that, either.

108 BELOVED OBJECTS

Wetsuit, Medium Large
THAILAND, 1988

Last night I had a spectacular dream. I was floating in space, far above the Earth. Looking down, I beheld our home planet in all its impossible beauty: the ochre of the deserts, the green of the jungles, the cerulean blue of the seas. But the oceans did not look opaque, as they do in pictures. They were transparent. From my great height I could see clear through them—down to the coral reefs, clouds of fish, and sulfur vents simmering on the ocean floor.

Inspired by the first launch of the SpaceX *Dragon* to the ISS, it made sense that my dream comingled space flight and scuba. I'd been inspired to take diving lessons by reading Arthur C. Clarke, who'd authored books set in both realms: from *The Coast of Coral* to *The Sands of Mars*. But Clarke knew he'd never make it into orbit. "The closest I'll ever come to weightlessness," he told me, "is scuba diving."

My most profound scuba memory is from a night dive, off the Philippine island of Mindoro. Divemaster Alan Nash and I took a motorboat out from the beach, and dropped into the sea at about 5 a.m. We were 60 feet down, surrounded by utter darkness. For the next 45 minutes, we explored a beautiful reef with powerful flashlights. Sharks and moray eels skittered through our beams, and the coral pulsed with living pink polyps.

As the sea began to lighten, Nash signaled that it was time to ascend. I was reluctant; but during our slow progress toward the surface, an astonishing thing happened. The water around us transformed from blue to green to fiery orange—as if the sea itself was aflame. What we were seeing, I realized, was sunrise: from within our prism of ocean.

The very instant our heads emerged into the air, the sun broke over the horizon. For an unforgettable moment, I felt the dizzying sensation of being on a moving planet: a rotating globe, spinning steadily among the stars.

Scuba diving is one of my passions. But with my post-surgery back issues, I may not be able to revisit that otherworldly realm, or sense of weightlessness, again.

I'm keeping my other wetsuit, just in case.

108 BELOVED OBJECTS

Small Fuzzy Rabbit
KENSINGTON, FEBRUARY 2019

My friend Marianne's annual Oscar party always includes a "Best Costume" contest. Though many come to the party, few take the competition seriously. But those who do, take it very seriously.

This year, there was no question of the winner. Marianne's friend Elsa arrived in truly majestic attire inspired by Queen Anne (as brilliantly portrayed by Olivia Colman) in *The Favourite*. As a nod to the Queen's menagerie of pet rabbits, the train of Elsa'a gown was filled with small toy bunnies. Upon her entrance she began tossing the furry favors around the room, dispensing them to her entranced subjects.

I caught one and handed it to M., my beautiful and idiosyncratic girlfriend, as a gift.

"I don't want it," she said bluntly. Seeing my wounded look she added, "I told you: I'm not interested in *things*. I'm interested in experiences."

This is true. For Christmas, she'd taken me to the ballet. My birthday gift was a visit to San Francisco's bizarre Gregangelo Museum, with its displays of hieroglyphs and aliens. She's set other boundaries as well. We see each other two nights a week, at most.

Prior to our relationship, M. had been following my work—"stalking" me, she says—for years, since she'd read *The Size of the World* and seen my solo show. "I wanted to know the man behind the myth," she said.

"Stick with the myth," I advised. Half-jokingly.

On our first date, we spread out my Tarot deck for a one-card reading. She drew The Lovers. Despite her cool outward persona, the card has proved prophetic. In our intimate encounters, M. is generous and responsive. I guess those count as "experiences."

Most of the women I've courted have been creative, sensitive, sometimes volatile. M. is stoic and logical; I often compare her to *Star Trek*'s Mr. Spock. She is sympathetic, but not empathetic. It would not have occurred to her that the gift of the toy rabbit was an effort to forge some kind of sentimental bond between us. Maybe she is capable of such bonds, but perhaps not. We may be as close as we'll get.

M. actually did win one of the contests at that party: She came closest to predicting the Oscar winners. She'd done this entirely by chance, barely looking at the entry form and checking off boxes at random. I may indeed be M.'s "favourite," but there also seems to be something random in the way our lives have intersected. And there may well come a day when, like that toy rabbit, I am ejected from her train.

108 BELOVED OBJECTS

Endings

Sequin-Studded Black Shoe
GREYHOUND ROCK, JUNE 2016

After weeks on a national book tour for *Grunt*, with radio interviews that sometimes began at 4 a.m., Mary Roach needed a break. When one of her events was scheduled for Bookshop Santa Cruz, she invited me to join her on the short road trip south and appear with her "in conversation."

I took the wheel of her blue Mini Cooper and drove us along Highway 1. We skirted the sharply defined edge of the continent, sharing mini-pretzels and nectarines. Mary's dearest wish was to stop for 15 minutes, somewhere, anywhere, and breathe the ocean air. I suggested Greyhound Rock: an obscure and beautiful county park, south of Año Nuevo and north of Davenport, where I'd spent many drug-addled afternoons during my half-hearted matriculation at UC Santa Cruz. One of the reasons I loved Greyhound Rock, I told her, was that it was a great place to find abalone fragments, hole-ridden rocks, and driftwood—objects I'd integrated into assemblages during my years as a visual artist.

We parked and followed a steep, lupine-lined path to the beach. It was intoxicating to be back on that nostalgic crescent of sand, watching the waves splinter against the eponymous offshore rock (which Mary insisted looked more like a crocodile). There wasn't much abalone or driftwood, but we found this shoe: A single black sequined flat, better suited to dancing than beach-walking.

How had it ended up here, amid the kelp and crab shells? Through lust, shipwreck, or distraction? How we longed for a QR code, a quick portal into the lonesome shoe's story.

Mary drew a good crowd at the bookshop, and kept her fans entranced with tales of stink bombs, maggot therapy, and penile reconstruction. And though I kept up my side of the conversation, my mind kept returning to this size 6 shoe. For every grain of sand at Greyhound Rock, there are a thousand stories that no one will hear.

108 BELOVED OBJECTS

Gentleman's Kangaroo Caddy
ARLINGTON, MA, 1959

From the time I was a child—maybe 5 or so—this ceramic boxing kangaroo caddy sat on my dad's dresser. He slipped rings onto the tail, placed tie pins and cufflinks in the pouch, and filled the open sack on the kangaroo's back with loose change.

My dad didn't leave many heirlooms. When he died in 1984, at the age of 54, this was the only possession of his that I "inherited."

Made in 1956 by Fine Enterprises this caddy was, in my mind, unique to my father. I'd never seen anything else like it. Imagine, then, my astonishment when, in 1994, the exact same kangaroo appeared as a prop in the film *Pulp Fiction*. The kangaroo's tail holds a gold watch, which Bruce Willis slips onto his wrist—right before shooting John Travolta. The sight of the kangaroo so disoriented me that I actually wondered, for a split second, if Quentin Tarantino had stolen it from my bedroom.

We live in an age when nothing is unique. Searching for the kangaroo on DuckDuckGo, I found dozens of them for sale—one of them holding a joey between its boxing gloves. Do you see those paws as boxing gloves? What else can they be? A nutty ex-girlfriend of mine thought they were boobs.

In one respect (the illusion of uniqueness), the kangaroo is like this book. *108 Beloved Objects* seemed a highly original idea when I first thought of it, years ago. Now there are plenty of object-oriented books—from *The Museum of Broken Relationships* to Roz Chast's *Can't We Talk About Something More Pleasant?* to *A History of Baseball in 100 Objects*. Now The Moth is doing something similar. I didn't even get to hold onto my number: e.g., *108 Objects from Flight 815*.

Oh well.

Even so, this is a tough one to let go of. Aside from its sentimental value, the caddy now holds *my* rings and tie pins. The sack on its back, once filled with pennies and dimes, is stuffed with my collection of buttons and badges (see *Man from U.N.C.L.E. pins*). What will become of all *that* "beloved" stuff? Should I include it with the kangaroo? Or save it for a sequel?

108 BELOVED OBJECTS

Virgin Mary
BASILICA DE LA CARIDAD DE COBRE, SANTIAGO, CUBA, 2013

In 2013, I led a group of travelers to Cuba. We were 17 in all, including myself, our local guide Joel, and my mother. Joel, usually vibrant, was despondent; his dog had just died, albeit at the impressive age of 19.

About 45 minutes from Santiago, near the island's southeastern tip, stands a cathedral built around a statue: The Virgin of Charity of El Cobre. Her legend is familiar to much of the Latin American world. About four centuries ago, three sailors were caught in a storm; Their small boat was tossed by wild waves. One of the three—an African slave child—wore a pendant of Mary, and prayed to the image. The sea miraculously calmed. In the distance, on the water's surface, the sailors spied a strange object. They rowed toward it, and found a statue of the Virgin riding on the swell.

Sunflowers are sold outside the basilica, along with innumerable replicas of the Virgin, set in plastic tubes and surrounded by flakes of *cobre* (copper)—for the Virgin protects miners as well as seamen. My mother and I bought a wreath of *girasoles* from a woman with a huge bun of white hair. We placed our flowers at the altar and lit narrow yellow candles, which we affixed reverently to a white slab crowded with many other flames.

Neither my observant Jewish mother nor I felt the slightest conflict, performing our ritual in a Catholic church beneath a grisly crucifix. We had done the same, separately and together, in Indian temples, at Buddhist shrines, in African mosques and European synagogues, since my brother's suicide in 1990. A desperate navigator of invisible tempests, Jordan had escaped his own tumultuous seascape the only way he could.

We lit another candle for the safety of our group, and one for my Mom's deceased parents. One also for my Dad, who died when I was 30. And a candle for Joel's dog.

We prayed. And then we emerged back into the jubilant Cuban sunlight, surrounded by sons and daughters, by sisters and brothers and jumping dogs, by fields of sunflowers, awash in an ocean of miracles.

108 BELOVED OBJECTS

Tsa-Tsa (Plaster & Cremation Ashes)
TIBET, 2002

On May 25th, 2000, two months short of his 52nd birthday, my friend Richard Kohn died of complications from bladder cancer. His cremation took place in California, and was witnessed by his wife Marianne and myself.

Rick was a devout Buddhist with a Ph.D. in Tibetan Studies. It is a tradition among Himalayan Buddhists, following a cremation, to mix the remaining ashes and bone fragments with consecrated clay or plaster, and create small devotional reliquaries called *tsa-tsa*. This one is in the form of a *stupa*, or shrine.

Tsa-tsa are sacred, but they are not rare. You can buy them on Amazon.

After Rick's death, Marianne had eight tsa-tsa made. In 2002, I carried one of them on my trek to Mount Kailash, and placed it amid the thousands of prayer flags and other offerings atop Drolma La: at 18,470', the highest pass on the main *kora* (pilgrimage route) around the holy mountain.

The tsa-tsa pictured here was given to me by a lama in Nepal. I don't know whose remains are within. The truth is, it doesn't matter. It could be any of us. We are all of us kin, molded from the same stellar elements.

But here's a thought: Almost 20 years to the day after Rick's death, George Floyd was killed by a police officer in Minneapolis. If George Floyd's ashes were in this small memorial, where might it best be placed?

If you have an answer, please let me send this to you.

108 BELOVED OBJECTS

Westclox Baby Ben Alarm Clock

NEW YORK 1997

This was my Nana's alarm clock.

Nana and I looked alike, laughed alike, even complained alike. She'd always been my favorite—and I hers. "You're my first!" she'd shrug, lavishing attention on me in front of my siblings and cousins.

Nana was well into her 80s, and still sharp, when I last visited her apartment. I was in my 40s—and though I was a travel writer, I didn't get to The Bronx very often.

Nana poured two cups of Sanka, and we moved into her living room. It had always looked the same: kitschy lamps, bowls of hard candies, and plush furniture "preserved" in old plastic slipcovers. I hated the slipcovers, but it had never occurred to me to take them off. That day, though—inspired by a recent visit to Tibet, and the Buddhist view of impermanence—I insisted.

At first Nana was terrified. But she quickly got into the act. Soon the yellowed vinyl was piled on the floor. She looked at her newly liberated furniture in disbelief. "Oh, my," she said, and lay down on the plush sofa. "Oh, my."

Nana was in her 90s when she moved into a nursing home. She was frail, and her memory was failing. I hadn't seen her in a couple of years, and I'd grown a beard. "Who are you?" she asked. She touched my face. "Do I know you?"

"It's Jeff, Nana! I've come from California to see you!" She looked puzzled, but continued to stroke my cheek. "I don't know who you are," she said at last. "But I know that I love you."

A few weeks later, my mother called me. "Nana won't let go," she said. "It's her time. But she's afraid to die." She put the phone to Nana's ear. "It's all right," I said. I told her how much I loved her. And then, to be sure she remembered me, I reminded her about the slipcovers.

Nana died that night, on the full moon of May: a day celebrated around the world as the anniversary of Buddha's birth. Some Buddhists believe that the merit of any action performed on this day is multiplied millions of times. If you step on a bug, it's as if you've wiped out the entire population of Topeka. But each act of kindness is a gift beyond measure.

Sometimes, shedding our skin is the kindest thing we can do for ourselves.

Spirit

I take no pride in saying so, but as a kid I was a bit of a thief. Like the much maligned magpie, I pilfered things—mostly shiny things—that caught my eye. And so it was that a few days after a junior high school chemistry class, during which the teacher had separated hydrogen from oxygen in a water beaker and demonstrated the properties of various other elements, I snuck into the science supply closet and stole a small plastic container of mercury.

Mercury is a deadly poison, a neurotoxin that can cause blindness, dementia, tremors. What did I know? It was more fun than Silly Putty, and a lot shinier. Anyone who's played with mercury—like after a fever thermometer dropped and shattered—understands the fascination. Tiny globs of pure silver slip across the palm of one's hand, uncatchable, seemingly with a life of their own.

Spirit, too, is alive, elusive, enthralling. When you try to corner it, it nimbly slips away. Spirit is an elemental part of who we are—but the way it appears depends on how it's held. A chorus of monks in a dark Tibetan temple; a ballroom dancer floating in the footlights; a solo climber, alone on the face of El Capitan. A morning run through Golden Gate Park, and the evening call to prayer in Shiraz. Spirit is alive, but it doesn't live in language. It lives in motion; in practice. And sometimes, the objects we keep can dance us back to the enchantment we felt at the time and place we found them.

About 20 years ago, at the beginning of the 21st century, mercury thermometers were banned in many states. Owning my small bottle of the element is probably illegal. Yet it's impossible to disown. As an artifact, the object recalls a time when I was fearless, selfish, and driven by a spirit of rebellion. Today, it's all metaphor—a proxy for an element in myself, and in you, that longs to be decanted, as bright and unvarnished as quicksilver.

108 BELOVED OBJECTS

Sand from a Tibetan Mandala
SAN FRANCISCO, 1991

In 1991, the Asian Art Museum of San Francisco opened a large exhibition called *Wisdom and Compassion: The Sacred Art of Tibet*. As part of the show, a group of six monks from the Dalai Lama's monastery in India created a magnificent sand mandala.

Like a painted mandala, a sand mandala is a visual representation of a divine space, used for meditation. It is created from millions of grains of colored sand, painstakingly tapped from small funnels onto a horizontal surface. The process takes weeks of work, and intense concentration. Though the final result is beautiful, it's also impermanent. After completion the entire mandala is swept up, collected, and poured as a sacred offering into a lake, river, or ocean. A small amount of the sand is retained.

As the Tibetan monks were completing their 6-foot-square sand mandala at the Asian Art Museum, a "deranged" woman in sneakers leaped suddenly into its center. Dancing maniacally, she obliterated the artwork. Onlookers screamed in anger and dismay; some even wept.

"I was smiling and laughing," commented Lobsang Samten, leader of the delegation of artist/monks.

I don't know exactly why Samten laughed. My guess is that he understood that he couldn't always dictate the terms of a sand mandala's impermanence. But aside from that, I'm not so sure the woman was deranged. I have my own theory.

Among the 159 artworks on display at the museum that spring were a number of ancient, secret *thangkas*: paintings of such overwhelming spiritual power that they are traditionally covered with silk brocade, to be viewed only by adept practitioners of Buddhist mysticism. Viewing them without the proper training, some lamas believe, can cause madness.

I've long wondered if the woman's only "crime" was being too deeply receptive to the artistic works on display. Was she guilty of vandalism, or a full participant in the process of creation/destruction? We will never know; the monks did not press charges.

108 BELOVED OBJECTS

Man from U.N.C.L.E. Pins
PLAINVIEW, 1967

During my final year of junior high school on Long Island, my friend Jeffrey and I were obsessed with *The Man from U.N.C.L.E.*, a television show inspired by the James Bond films but lacking the urbane sophistication of, say, *The Saint* or *I Spy*.

I was 13, unhappy, and deeply impressionable. My friend and I amassed a collection of *U.N.C.L.E.*-inspired guns and other toy props. But Jeffrey went so far as to write a hopeful, full-length screenplay for an episode of the show—a flight of genius so far beyond my capacities that it forever separated us intellectually. (He later became a well-known film producer, and wrote and directed several films of his own.)

My own skill was in petty theft, and I was able to pilfer a roll of magnesium tape from our high school lab. Mg tape was often used as a prop on *The Man from U.N.C.L.E.*; hidden on the person of agent Napoleon Solo or Illya Kuryakin, it flared superhot when ignited, melting locks and doorknobs, and allowing quick entries or escapes.

What I personally needed to escape from was my adolescence. I was a weakling and a coward. My useless tape and plastic model of Solo's famous gun (so novel and realistic that MGM was investigated under suspicion of producing genuine firearms) allowed me to hide behind the role of a self-assured superspy—when I wasn't being chased home after school.

Even today, having evolved into the antipode of my boyhood self, remnants of that secret agent alter-ego remain. I'll pack my electric bass into my car, wondering if my neighbors suspect anything. I'll travel away on a writing assignment, elusive about my destination. I'll pretend I am who I am not, not quite certain I want to be who I actually am.

108 BELOVED OBJECTS

Brass Water Tank Faucet

KHAO I DANG, THAILAND, 1979

The little Thai island of Koh Samui was still undeveloped in 1979, reachable only by ferry from the southern city of Surat Thani. I was sharing a straw hut on a coconut-pocked beach with Dorothy, a newly minted M.D. who I'd been traveling with since we had met, nine months before, in Greece.

How had we learned about the civil war in erupting in Cambodia? Radio? A local newspaper? In any event, as soon as the news reached us, Dorothy insisted we return to Bangkok and volunteer with the UNHCR: The United Nations High Commissioner for Refugees, tasked with housing the tens of thousands of Cambodians fleeing the madness of Pol Pot's regime.

We left Bangkok for Aranyaprathet, on the Thai/Cambodian border, on November 21st. The next morning the 12 volunteers in our group were assigned tasks, based on our skills. Dorothy was assigned to the medical tent. Reluctant to pass out plastic buckets or soap, I told the UNHCR supervisor that, as a sculptor, I possessed some basic engineering skills.

He regarded me warily. "What kinds of 'skills?'"

"Well, I've designed playgrounds," I offered, "and a few fountains." What I *didn't* tell him is that none of these structures had been built.

"Okay," he nodded. "You're on water."

"Water?" I awaited a specific assignment.

"Yeah. The water systems. This camp is going to have 10 sectors, and each sector will need at least six water areas. So we have to build a lot of them and we have to do it *fast*—because we're expecting about 80,000 people within the next three days."

"What kinds of systems are talking about?"

"The whole works. Big metal water tanks, gravel, drainage, faucets."

"Umm...Sure," I told him, stammering. "Who do I report to? Who do I see?"

"*See?*" He looked at me with incomprehension. "You don't *see* anyone. I told you the problem. It's your job to solve it."

And I did.

108 BELOVED OBJECTS

12" World Globe
SANTA BARBARA, 1981

There was a restless gap between my first trip to Nepal in 1979 and my Rotary Fellowship return to Kathmandu in 1983. During that hiatus, working as a writer, editor, and artist in Santa Barbara, Nepal became an obsession. Getting back to that chaotic Hindu kingdom was all I could think about. Sometimes, the inland peaks of the Santa Ynez range would fool my eye and appear, for an instant, like the Himalaya. Whenever that happened, my heart skipped a beat.

During my 1979 visit to Nepal, I'd become fascinated with the ingenious prayer technology invented by Tibetan Buddhists. Prayer flags stampeded on long lines in the wind, sending their mantras heavenward; prayer wheels packed with blessings were spun by hand, clockwise, on the pilgrimage paths circling temples and shrines. Larger prayer wheels were anchored in streams, animated by water power. The prayers within were always the same. *Om Mani Padme Hun*: the Jewel in the Heart of the Lotus.

ཨོཾ་མ་ཎི་པདྨེ་ཧཱུྃ

In 1982 I had what I thought was a genius idea: turn a world globe into a prayer wheel. The concept of using the Earth's own rotation as a force of spiritual good was entrancing. I traced out the Tibetan invocation, planning to paint it onto a world globe I'd found at Goodwill.

But there was one problem: the direction of the planet's spin. Viewed from the customary orientation, with the North Pole on top, the Earth turns to the right: counterclockwise. Prayer wheels, though, must always spin clockwise. This led me to wonder: From a Buddhist perspective, could our long-held model of the Earth's position in space be upside down?

Imagine the implications of correcting that Eurocentric error. What if we simply inverted our world view, turned over our maps, and placed Antarctica at the *top* of the world? Maybe humanity's dysfunctional relationship with our home planet would also reverse. Maybe, at last, we'd have a prayer.

108 BELOVED OBJECTS

Squeaky Buddha
OAKLAND, 1990

For what do I need a squeaky Buddha?
Maybe to remind me to squeak less?

Chokyi Nyima, the Tibetan *Rinpoche*[3] I studied with in Kathmandu, was an early adopter. Even during the 1990s, as he sat on his raised dais during the Saturday morning teachings, a cell phone was always by his side. Whenever it rang—which was often—he'd stop in the middle of the teaching and take the call. The conversations might go on for a while, as the assembled students sat on the carpeted floor and waited.

Personally, I hate it when a conversation is interrupted by a phone call. It's hard to understand the compulsion to answer. Why is a ringing phone any different from someone just walking up and poking your shoulder to get your attention? "Sorry, I have to take this call." Do you? One time in a hundred, there may be an urgent matter to attend to. But for some crazy reason, that's always the assumption.

The Rinpoche, to his credit, gave every caller his undivided attention. Meanwhile, his students were ignored. As we sat in silence listening to one side of his lively conversation, we engaged in a contest of patience. Not a soul expressed irritation. There was a placid, knowing smile on everyone's face. Well, almost everyone's. I tried to see it their way: This was about acceptance, equanimity, letting go of expectations. It was an opportunity to empty our minds of ego-generated thoughts. It was, in fact, a teaching.

And honestly? It was also kind of rude.

Squeak, squeak, squeak.

---

3 *An honorific meaning "precious one," used to address incarnate lamas.*

108 BELOVED OBJECTS

Tefillin
PLAINVIEW, NY, 1967

You shall put these words of mine on your heart and on your soul; and you shall tie them for a sign upon your arm, and they shall be as totafot between your eyes.

- Deuteronomy 11:18

One summer afternoon, as I emerged from the subway at Times Square, I was accosted by two young, bearded members of the Lubavitch sect, an Orthodox/Hasidic branch of Judaism. With unerring "Jew-dar," they knew I was of the tribe. The men peppered me with questions about my life, my career, and my relationship to the Jewish religion. Then they thrust a pair of *tefillin* in my face.

"Let us put these on your body! Affirm your Judaism!"

Tefillin come as a pair; they consist of two small wooden boxes holding the scripture above, and long leather thongs with which to wrap the boxes around one's head and arms. These were given to me at my bar mitzvah, at age 13. In my opinion the wearing of tefillin is one of the strangest of Orthodox Judaism's rituals. And though I love many Jewish rites—like the beautiful Passover Seder, and the deep introspection of the "Days of Awe" that fall between Rosh Hashanah and Yom Kippur—putting on tefillin seems utterly ridiculous to me. I said so.

"Listen to you," one of the men said derisively. "You call yourself a travel writer? If you were in India or Peru, and were invited to take part in a local ritual, would you refuse? Of course not! Yet here we are, in the city where you were born, and you won't honor a ritual from your own religion!"

They had me there. Yet I continued to resist. They did not relent. Ultimately, I realized that my only escape route was to let them affix the tefillin to my body. I stood there near the entrance to the subway, wrapped up in these things, feeling like a fool. My taskmasters beamed with delight, and asked if I wanted a photograph. I did not.

There is a difference between being invited to join a ritual and being coerced, by mockery and manipulation, to do so. I'll never wear tefillin again. But if you feel a connection with the Divine when you strap these wooden objects to your body, please, take them home—with my blessing.

108 BELOVED OBJECTS

Spirit

Avalokiteshvara Statue
NEPAL, 1990

Known by many names in Buddhist and Hindu cultures the world over, Avalokiteshvara is a form of Chenrezig, the many-eyed god of compassion. Chenrezig is a *bodhisattva*: an individual who is qualified to enter nirvana, but has chosen instead to abide on the Earth, among its billions of imperfect beings, until each of us is liberated from suffering.

In 1996 I had the great good fortune to spend an hour interviewing Tenzin Gyatso, the 14th Dalai Lama, at his home in India. Revered by the Tibetan people, the Dalai Lama is believed to be a direct reincarnation of Chenrezig himself. The subject of our meeting was popular science—especially as it related to *Star Trek*, which the Dalai Lama, himself an outer space aficionado, had watched gleefully as a young man. Our interview appears in *Future Perfect: How Star Trek Conquered Planet Earth*. But the book leaves out this anecdote.

After we exchanged greetings, the Dalai Lama and I moved to an L-shaped sofa with a small table at the bend. I placed my pen on the table. As the Dalai Lama sat down, he swept his maroon robe over his shoulder and, accidentally, across the table. The thick cloth sent my pen flying. It hit the floor and rolled under another couch, across from us.

Before I could move or utter a word of protest, the Dalai Lama dived onto the floor. His upper body disappeared under the nearby couch, stirring up a cloud of dust bunnies.

"Your Holiness!" I cried. "Please get up! I'll get the pen!"
"No, no, no!" he boomed, his head completely out of sight. "It is my responsibility!"

I learned more about the Dalai Lama in that moment than from any book I'd read. I tried to imagine then-Pope John Paul II in the same situation; it was impossible.

This 19-inch-tall wooden statue of the god of compassion has stood on my bedroom dresser for 30 years. It always reminds me of that moment, and of the meaning of humility.

108 BELOVED OBJECTS

Blue Conga Ornament
SAN FRANCISCO, 1985

The Nobel Prize-winning physicist Richard Feynman (1918-1988) is famous for many things, including his proof of why the Space Shuttle *Challenger* exploded (a frozen O-ring). When he was introduced at academic functions, his hosts often added the fact that he played the bongos.

"It is odd," Feynman mused. "On the infrequent occasions when I have been called upon in a formal place to play the bongo drums, the introducer never seems to find it necessary to mention that I also do theoretical physics. I believe that is probably because we respect the arts more than the sciences."

Feynman made that remark in 1965. I wonder if it's still true. I do know that when I add science-y anecdotes to this project, it feels like I'm diverging from my more art-y personal stories. But the sciences define me as much as my writing, relationships, and travels. Growing up during the Space Age, I was fascinated by sci-fi, chemistry sets, dissections, and astronomy. Those obsessions led to my lifelong friendship with Arthur C. Clarke, my work at the San Francisco Exploratorium, and my brief but exhilarating stint as a speech writer for Buzz Aldrin.

Feynman and I looked strangely alike in our late 30s. And like the late physicist, I love to drum. Somehow, mysteriously, I acquired my first African hide drum at 10. Bongos, rattles, and an *ashiko* drum occupy a corner of my small flat. Mindful of my neighbors, I rarely play them.

As for this tree ornament: It was purchased as a totem, a reminder to do more drumming. I tried. I even took a conga class. But I cannot, in good conscience, drum in my thin-walled Oakland fourplex. My new electric bass, however, is a different story. I plug in headphones, and play guilt-free. And my weekly lessons are teaching me about music theory, a science in its own right.

But a full-body immersion in rhythm is a state beyond the rational confines of scientific thought. That's why I still feel a pang when I watch videos of a beatific Feynman playing the bongos. Not because I gave up drumming, but because these clips show me what a fully integrated spirit—a human at home in two worlds—looks like.

Ah, Feynman. How I would have relished even a single lesson with you—on any subject.

108 BELOVED OBJECTS

Plaster Venus

NEW PALTZ, NEW YORK, 1976

A friend who'd won a small role in a Woody Allen film told me the most difficult thing about working with the eccentric director.

"I could never tell if he was being sincere or sarcastic," she said.

I asked for an example. "The cameras would roll. I'd make my entrance into a scene, and when the shot was over Woody would give me a totally deadpan look and say, 'Nice entrance.'"

My brother Jordan had a similarly opaque mien. He was three years and three months younger than me, but as I'd taken a long break between my second and third years at university we were college students at pretty much the same time. Opposite coasts, though: While I was at UC Santa Cruz, Jordan was at SUNY New Paltz.

One winter, I flew to New York to visit him on campus. Though his major was linguistics he was taking a studio art class, and invited me to attend. Everyone was given a toaster-sized block of plaster and a set of chisels. I was not a stranger to art, but my sculptural work had all involved assemblage: nailing, screwing, fitting, and gluing together pieces of metal, fur, wood, and cloth. I knew nothing about carving.

Still, I'd read *The Agony and the Ecstasy*—Irving Stone's biographical novel about the life of Michelangelo. There was a figure within that plaster block, waiting to be released by the hand of an artist. I attacked the plaster without inhibition. By the time the class ended, this rough but recognizable creature had been liberated from the stone.

Jordan had succeeded in whittling his own plaster block down to a grain of its original size, with no discernable result. But he took a step over to my workbench, picked up this primitive figure, and turned it in his hand.

"A bold achievement, by an irrepressible talent," he said, moving barely a muscle in his face. A compliment, or withering sarcasm? I'll never know.

108 BELOVED OBJECTS

Small Demon Mask
SRI LANKA, 1984

Late one night, as I walked along Sri Lanka's west coast, I was drawn away from the seashore by the distant beating of drums. As I approached its source the sound swelled, filling the humid air with locomotive force. Soon I found myself at the edge of a crowded, torch-lit clearing. The drummers crouched on one side, illuminated by torches, entranced by their own rhythms.

An exorcism had begun. The elderly victim sat off-center, wrapped in a white shawl. A tightly-bound rooster lay by his side. The rite was being performed, I learned, to free the man from recurrent headaches: the curse of a demon.

The ceremony continued through the night, a riot of sound and fire. The exorcist whirled batons of flame; he then donned a series of masks and, showing impressive theatrical chops, enacted a series of scenes and dances. He carried the crowd to manic laughter, then jarred us back to earth with fearsome changes in temperament.

As the stars vanished, the shaman completed his ritual. He ducked briefly behind a canvas curtain—and sprang out again with a roar. Eyes popping, tongue extended, he leaped into the air. Torches flared, and the drums exploded in a nearly deafening cadence. With all the evil power condensed in his body the shaman/demon, exorcised and rampant, threw himself upon his sacrificial prize. Horrible squawks pierced the air as he tore the rooster apart. Feathers flew, blood spattered, and the sun broke over the nearby sea.

Nearly four decades have passed, but the events of that night return to haunt me. Ever since publishing a book about my brother's suicide in 2010, I too have felt possessed. It's as if some vengeful aspect of Jordan, resentful of his portrayal in *Snake Lake*, has entered my body to share a taste of his affliction. I often think about how far I would go to evict that demon—if I could convince myself that such a rite made sense. But I wonder what sort of sacrifice I might be willing to offer; my cock is not the prize it once was.

108 BELOVED OBJECTS

White Nautical Rope
SANTA BARBARA, 1981

After leaving my job as Cultural Editor at the *Santa Barbara News & Review*, I indulged two great passions: graphic art and sculpture. My 3D artworks were interactive, made of materials that invited touch and manipulation. As mentioned in the *Brass Bells* story, I thought of them as mini-playgrounds: akin to those "busy boxes" that keep drooling toddlers occupied in the back seats of cars.

Shopping for materials was always fun—whether in Goodwill, scrap shops, hardware stores, or chandleries. This short length of ¾-inch-thick cotton rope is all that remains of a sculpture exhibited in an art gallery on Santa Barbara's State Street. Webbed and anchored tightly to the walls and ceiling, the rope and brass piece held a lot of tension, and vibrated with potential energy. It was called *David Answers Goliath's Challenge*.

Most classical paintings of David and Goliath show the scene after Goliath is felled, as David prepares to sever the warrior's head. For me, though, the defining moment in that story is when David—an anonymous shepherd—steps out of the crowd, volunteering to take on the giant.

I believe there are moments in all our lives when we have an opportunity to do something that hints at the heroic; an act that will define us from that point forward. Usually, we decline. But David... Well, he had total confidence in that sling. And having seen slings wielded by yak herders in Tibet, I can attest to their astounding accuracy and pistol-like power.

About two years after the above mentioned gallery show, I gave up visual art for writing. I'm not sure I've ever done anything heroic. But I have learned that for a writer, launching a book is like slinging a stone at a huge and intimidating target, never at all sure—unlike David—if it will hit or miss.

108 BELOVED OBJECTS

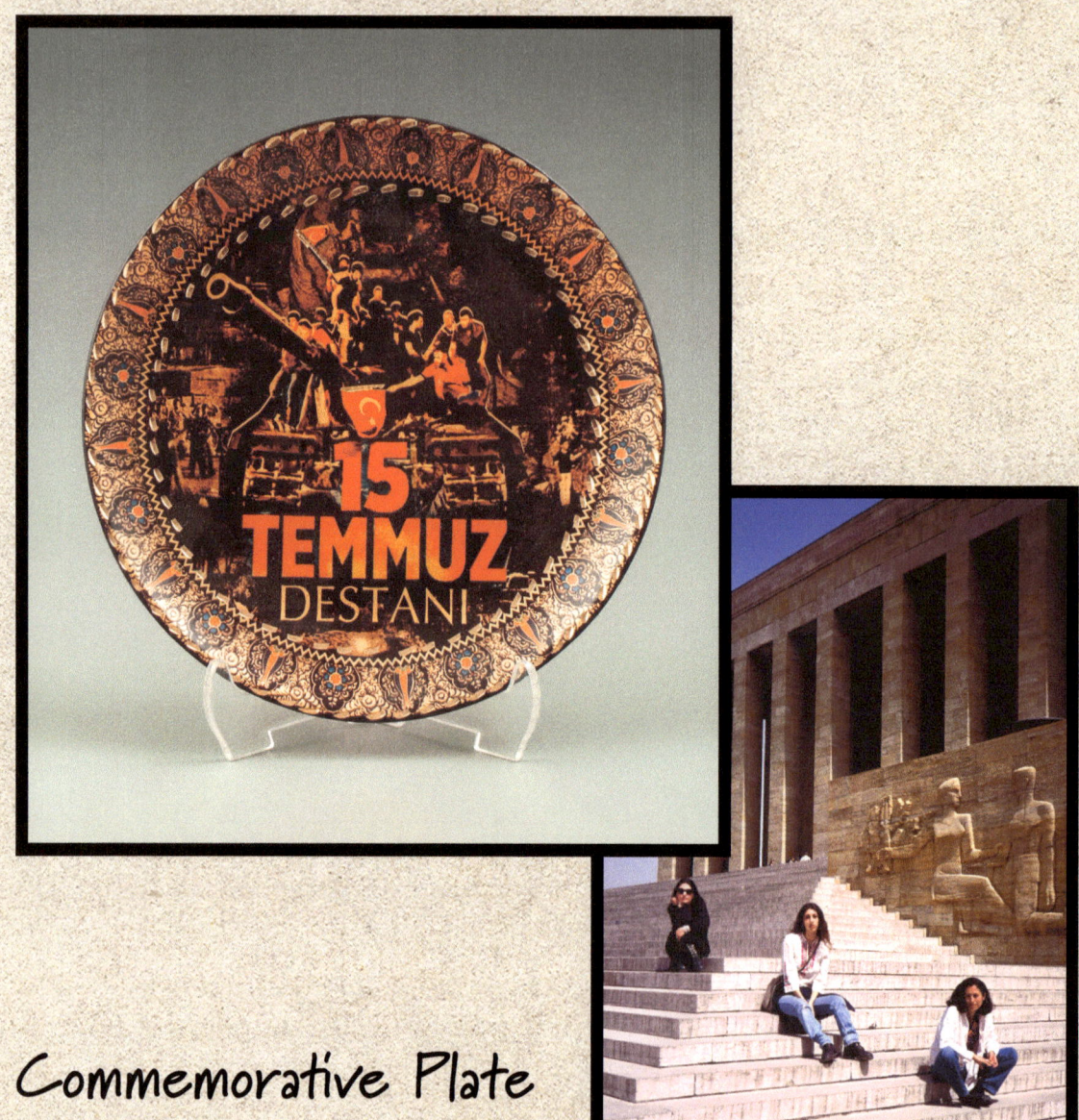

Commemorative Plate

TURKEY, 2017

The three women laughing together at the café in Ankara were so beautiful that I never dreamed of approaching them. It was a hot day in the spring of 1994, and I was having an espresso while waiting for the "luxury" bus for Iğdir, near the Turkey/Iran border. My plan was to bribe my way through the check post, and travel across Iran to Pakistan. I had no idea how foolish an idea that was, but I'd find out soon enough.

Spirit

Abruptly, one of the women—dark-haired, green-eyed, dreamily exotic—stood up and strolled, head held high with self-conscious boldness, to my table. "We would like you to join us," she declared.

Her name was Fatima. She and her equally striking friends, Servin and Jalé, had guessed I was Milanese. They were disappointed by my true pedigree. But Fatima was reading *In the House of the Spirits*, and Jalé was halfway through *The Stories of Eva Luna*—and when I mentioned that I knew Isabel Allende, it was better than being Italian. I delayed my journey to the border.

The following day the three women, all in their late teens, took me to Anitkabir. This is the mausoleum of Kemal Ataturk, the nation's beloved first president. Along with unifying Turkey, Ataturk was a progressive despot who had kept Turkey from being carved up by the Allied powers after World War I. He vowed to keep Turkey secular, and guaranteed equal rights for women.

Fatima carried a bottle of vodka in her purse; we nursed it as we toured the crypt and museum. When we left the memorial and sat on the broad marble steps, she and her two friends burst into tears.

"We need him," Jalé sobbed. "We need him *now*."

* * *

They had reason to be worried. Even in 1994, right-wing forces were rising in Turkey, threatening the nation's progressive policies and constitutional rejection of *shari'a*, Islamic law.

Today, under President Recep Tayyip Erdoğan's increasingly corrupt and conservative government, many people fear that Turkey—long the land bridge between the East and West—might regress to the pious oppressions of the Ottoman Empire. But millions of Turks still revere Ataturk, and embrace secularism. On July 15th, 2016, there was a coup d'état, by the Turkish Army, against Erdoğan.

The uprising failed. But one year later, on the anniversary of the coup, millions of people took to the streets to recall the event and protest Erdoğan's rule.

Did Jalé, Servin, and Fatima, now in their 40s, join in the demonstrations? I don't know. I wasn't there—but this plate, and my fearless friend Dwayne, were.

Watermelon Seed Purse

BURMA, 2003

In July of 1996 I published an op-ed in *The Washington Post*, urging fellow travelers to "vote with their wings" and use their collective economic power to advance human rights. Do not visit Burma, I wrote, while the nation's legally elected president— Aung San Suu Kyi—is under arrest, and a brutal military dictatorship in power. I was asking a lot. Burma is a fascinating country, and the birthplace of *vipassana*: the "insight meditation" tradition that has becoming so popular in the West.

Seven years after my op-ed was published, there was a brief period during which the junta's restrictions were eased. In 2003, *Yoga Journal* sent me to Burma with a question: Was it at last conscionable to visit a country where, since 1988, tourist dollars had been used to arm and support a murderous regime?

Burma was still under the thumb of the military during my visit, and free speech was suppressed. Still, Aung San Suu Kyi was no longer imprisoned. But any notion of a meaningful change in the state's policies was extinguished during my visit to Mandalay.

I'd spent the morning visiting temples and monasteries, and climbing long, covered stairways toward the spires of golden pagodas. Inside the temples sat grinning buddhas, surrounded by donation boxes and blinking Christmas lights. The paths between the shrines were lined with tiny stalls. Some sold fresh watermelon; at others, squatting women sold heavy little purses made of beaded watermelon seeds.

I returned to Mandalay before sunset. That evening, the American Mission (there was no U.S. Embassy in Burma at that time) was hosting an outdoor concert on the grounds of a Russian-owned luxury hotel. The event was sponsored by "Voices America," a State Department program that brings American performers abroad. That night's concert promised to be groundbreaking: Jazz singer Deborah Carter and pianist Mike del Ferro would be joined by five local musicians, all playing traditional instruments. The Burmese and Americans had been rehearsing together for days.

Less than an hour before the show, the hotel received a terse call from the military: Any Burmese musician who took part in the concert would be arrested.

Hundreds of Burmese, the elite of Mandalay society, had already gathered on folding chairs in the hotel garden, dressed in their finest *longyis* and sparkling gowns. Hearing the news, many whispered and fidgeted nervously; plainclothes police surely lurked among us. But silence descended as Carmen Martinez, the American Chief of Mission, strode onto the raised wooden stage.

"Tonight we had hoped that you would experience a fusion of traditional American jazz and Burmese harmonies," she announced. "Unfortunately, that won't happen—because our wonderful Mandalay musicians have been forbidden to perform by order of the government. But we," Martinez stated, "will proceed with our own program."

As the crowd digested this news, Deborah Carter—a vibrant African American woman raised in Hawaii and Japan—walked silently into the spotlight. Her voice was choked with emotion. "Here is a song once sung by the slaves in America," she said, "in hopes of the day their oppression would end."

Surrounded by silenced Burmese drums and harps, Carter raised the microphone. She began to sing, her words ringing into the dusk:

> *Hold on, just a little while longer*
> *Hold on, just a little while longer*
> *Hold on, just a little while longer*
> *Everything will be all right.*

How times change. Who would have dreamed that today, a quarter-century later, Suu Kyi—now one of her country's leaders—would face global condemnation for her silence around the government's genocide of south Burma's Rohingya Muslims?

Burma is still a beautiful, enchanting country. But the dollars spent by visitors are again paying for the cudgels, cattle prods, and bullets the government uses against its own people.

108 BELOVED OBJECTS

Spirit

Black Granite Rock
MOUNT KAILASH, TIBET, 2002

Every 12 years the Tibetan zodiac repeats itself, cycling through a menagerie of mythical beasts and barnyard animals. Most auspicious is the Year of the Horse—the year of my birth. Every Horse Year, the merit gained by a pilgrimage to Tibet's Mount Kailash is multiplied many times. And so, in 2002, I joined thousands of Buddhists, Hindus, and other seekers on the *kora* (devotional clockwise circuit) circling the holy mountain.

The journey to Kailash is torturous, a karmic crucible that reduces pilgrims to their essence. True to form, it was among the most difficult and despairing experiences of my life. Though the mountain is utterly magnificent, and the spiritual power of the raw, stony, high-altitude kora left me awe-struck, I faced an awful challenge: The only other traveler in my tiny group was Helga, a deeply troubled and likely bipolar German woman.

Helga took it into her head that I was a loathsome presence, surrounded by a "black aura." She warned our timid Nepali guide and cooks—whom she plied with sex, clothing, and promises of education abroad—to provide me no services. Her demonic mien terrified them, and with awkward apologies to me they obeyed. I responded with what I imagined was required of me on this Buddhist enterprise: compassion and equanimity.

The geology of Kailash is hallucinatory. Each stone—each cell of the landscape—embodies the entire mountain, like the grains of a hologram. I picked up many rocks but kept few, placing most atop the high cairns and prayer-carved *mani* walls that marked passes, gompas, and other significant stations along the route.

One rock—black granite, flecked with white—became my touchstone. Raised to the surface despite unimaginable obstacles, it became a symbol of power and perseverance: the inner strength I'd need to complete my Horse Year pilgrimage with integrity.

During our three-week trek—over the Nepali border into Tibet, past Lake Manasarovar, around Mount Kailash and back—Helga's craziness persisted. I was abused, ignored, and treated as a contaminant. But on the final day of the trip, gripping my stone, I finally fathomed the meaning of my test. Not all adversaries can be treated with docility. I raised my sword, and (metaphorically, but decisively) slew the demoness.

On my return to Kathmandu, I asked my 14-year-old goddaughter what I should call my account of this strange and terrible journey. She answered, unhesitating, with a brilliant bit of word play: "Black Kora."

108 BELOVED OBJECTS

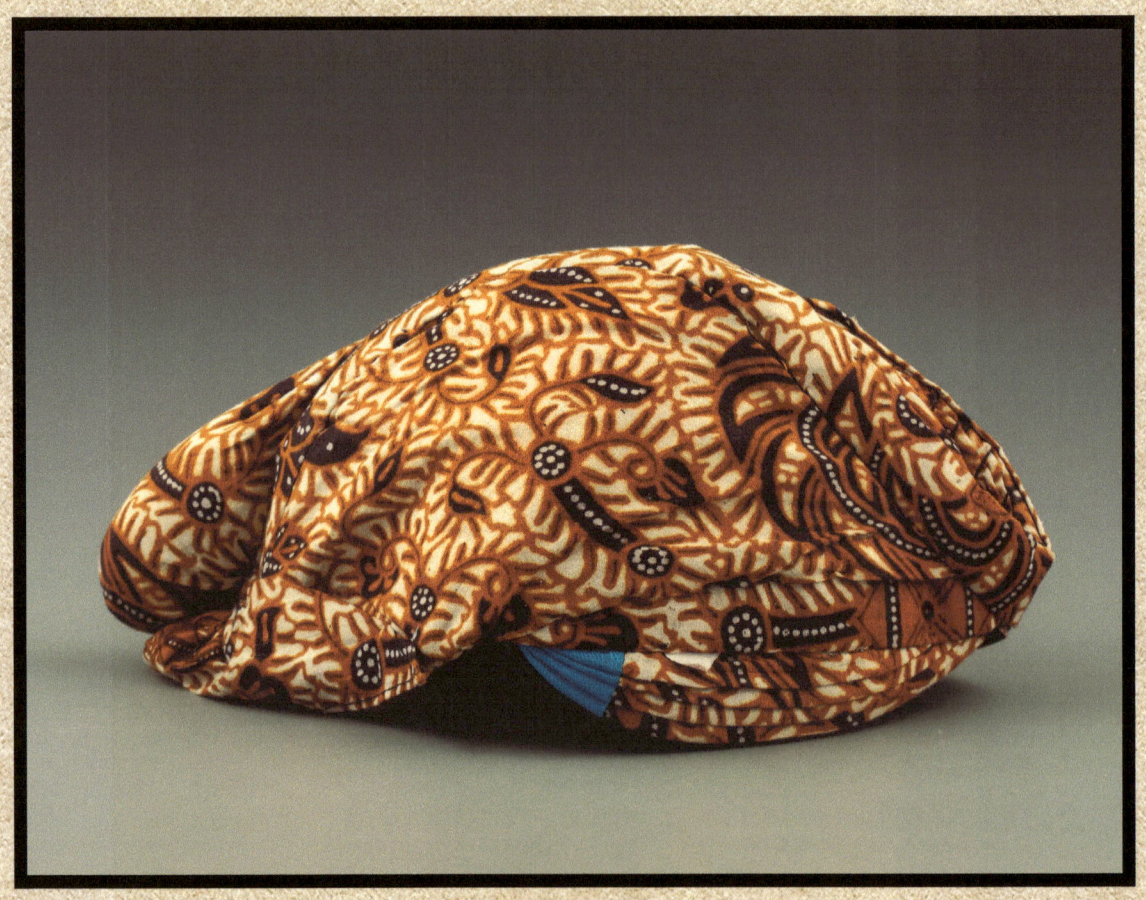

Traditional Blangkon (Royal Court Hat)
JAVA, 1984

Near midnight in Yogyakarta, as the sidewalk vendors packed their wares, I came upon a group of bicycle rickshaw drivers. They squatted on straw mats, laughing and shouting at a flickering light on a veranda. The source of the light, I discovered, was a black-and-white television—playing an American cop show. Despite the incomprehensible story and alien tongue, the men cheered like rugby fans at every change of scene.

A few hours earlier, the sight would have baffled me. That very evening, though, I'd attended my first *wayang kulit* performance.

Wayang kulit are flat, carved-leather puppets that "perform" behind a backlit screen. Their shadows loom and dissolve, the audience spellbound by myths drawn from 3,000 years of Hindu lore. The art itself is almost as old—even in modern Yogya, few men are more revered than a skillful *dalang*, or puppet master. As he manipulates the heroes, villains, and clowns—providing narration, dialogue, action, even special effects—the dalang assumes a god-like role.

The performance I attended was still underway when I left. It would continue until dawn, to a live soundtrack provided by the hypnotic, ceaseless rhythms of a gamelan orchestra.

One thing surprised me. Though I'd expected the audience to be enraptured by the ghostly shadows, the screen was arranged so that the *blangkon*-capped dalang—sitting cross-legged amidst his racks of meticulously crafted puppets—was in plain view. The spectators were as fascinated by the dalang as by the shadow show itself.

It was later that evening that I came upon the assembly of *becak* drivers, riveted to their TV show. Pausing for a moment, I beheld the bizarre hijinks of the police drama through their eyes. How outrageous those foreign wayang "puppets" must have appeared—and how mysterious the dalang!

Día de los Muertos Catrina Figure
MEXICO, 1984

In October of 1984, *Islands* magazine assigned me to visit Janitzio—a tiny island in the middle of Michoacán's Lake Pátzcuaro—to write about their beautiful Day of the Dead celebration. It was the first time I'd heard of *Día de los Muertos*, and the timing was eerie: My father had died of a sudden heart attack, at 54, in September.

Janitzio's all-night ritual was held in the island's old hilltop cemetery. The intensity of the tradition—illuminated by candles and music, and fragrant with tobacco, frying fish, and liquor—mesmerized me. I fell in love with the icons of the holiday: the candy skulls, chains of marigolds, and *pan de los muertos* ("bread of the dead"), and especially the elegant Catrina: a worldly, materialistic Mexican woman dressed in European haute couture, reduced to a dancing skeleton.

Though Catrina originated in the early 20th century (as a satire of upper-class pretensions by Mexican artist José Guadalupe Posada), I had seen a similar image in Nepal. *Citipati* is a Buddhist image of two gleefully dancing skeletons, male and female, celebrating release from their bodies.

After my father died, I discovered, among his private notes, a confession that he suffered from severe depression. He'd hidden it well, beneath a thick layer of joking, flirtation, and bonhomie. But it all came together when I realized with a shock that I'd never seen him dance. Not once. Not even at my bar mitzvah.

I thought about him often during that all-night ceremony in Janitzio's candlelit graveyard. He departed this world when I was 30, but I barely knew him. I wondered, as I sat among the tombstones, who my father really was beneath his charming disguise—and where he might be now. Maybe it's true, as a Hindu sage once said, that "Dying is like taking off a tight shoe."

I hope so. Maybe my father is dancing at last, spinning Catrina in his bony arms.

108 BELOVED OBJECTS

Ceramic Monkey Saltshaker
KENSINGTON CA, 2000

Wandering the souks of Fes in 1994, I bought a fez for my dear friend Richard Kohn.

Rick was an anachronism, fiercely beloved by his friends. A Ph.D. in Tibetan Studies, he also possessed an encyclopedic knowledge of fine cigars, haberdashery, bebop jazz, caviar, and film noir. And he was a brilliant documentarian. His 1987 film *Lord of the Dance, Destroyer of Illusion*, was a poetic visual journey through an ancient Tibetan dance ritual, narrated by Richard Gere.

In 1995, Rick was diagnosed with cancer. A year before the disease took his life, he gave me this salt-and-pepper set. The pepper shaker got broken somehow. I don't recall.

A few days after Rick died, his wife Marianne and I were sitting at her kitchen table in Kensington. "My friends ask me if they can do anything, if there is anything I want," she said despondently. "But there's nothing they can do." She raised her voice. *"I want my husband back."*

At that instant, we heard a crash in the living room. Marianne and I looked at each other, dumbfounded. We stood, traversed the dining room, and saw Rick's most prized headwear—a vintage explorer's pith helmet—resting on the living room floor. It was overturned, like a Buddhist begging bowl. Beside it lay an antique Nepali hotel ledger, splayed open to a sign-in page with a single name inscribed: mine. I'd written it there years ago, as a joke.

Nothing evident could have dislodged these objects from their place of display: a high, broad shelf in the room's enormous bookcase. The object placed next to the helmet—the Moroccan fez—remained unmoved.

We will never know if my friend was indulging in a final bit of monkey business during his journey through the *bardo*, that mysterious interregnum between death and rebirth. But the following day a solicitation letter, addressed to Rick, arrived from a book club neither Marianne nor I had ever heard of. A membership card was enclosed, admitting Richard Kohn into "The Reincarnation Library."

108 BELOVED OBJECTS

One Hundred and Eight Books
OAKLAND, 2019

Every year, in preparation for the Burning Man gathering in Nevada's Black Rock Desert, a chosen architect gets to design the Temple: a phantasmagorical sanctuary dedicated to love, loss, and memory. Towering above the alkaline dust of the ancient playa, the Temple is traditionally made of reclaimed wood. Despite its humble origins, it briefly ranks among the most beautiful structures on Earth. For on the final day of the event—as tens of thousands of participants watch in silence—it is consumed by flames.

I've long imagined designing the Temple, using a different form of recycled wood: the books that have touched our lives. All of them: *Good Night Moon* and chemistry textbooks, spy thrillers, Harry Potter novels and celebrity memoirs, Mexico guidebooks, *The Joy of Cooking* and *I, Robot*, cheesy bestsellers and signed first editions, art books and coffee table tomes, even the sad books we began but never finished. For many of us, our life sum of books would number in the thousands.

Of all the objects in this volume, books are the easiest to reproduce. There is almost no real need of a hard copy any more, although we do live in a shoulder season where actual, physical books make good gifts and remain symbols of our proclivities, education, intelligence, and taste.

There is no backstory linking the 108 books (treated here as a single object) that I have chosen to give away. They have been assembled randomly, and will be dispatched in kind. Together, they represent a narrow slice of a lifetime's worth of curiosity, entertainment, and intention. Some I sincerely meant to read—like *The Accidental Fundraiser* and *Don Quixote*. There are science fiction anthologies and travel narratives, memoirs and novels. Others (*Flavius Josephus*, *Zombies on Kilimanjaro*) were gifts. Many (*The Merck Manual*, Merriam Webster's *Encyclopedia of Literature*) have been made obsolete by the Internet.

Larry Harvey, the visionary co-creator of Burning Man, died in April 2018. In 2019, artist Dana Albany built a memorial pagoda to Harvey on the Black Rock playa. It rested atop four pillars of books—a tribute to the founder's identity as a devoted bookworm.

If I were to design a Temple of my own, using the towers of books that have passed through my hands, what might it look like? I think immediately of Gaudi's Sagrada Familia: something surreal yet coherent, sacred but irreverent, and slouching endlessly toward completion—the finial topped by this book itself.

Afterword

We see the offerings on curbs and corners: the objects people no longer need to live with. A vintage toaster oven; Dr. Seuss books once relished by children who have graduated to Harry Potter; a colorful Mexican *sarape*, folded over a cardboard box filled with used sneakers. During our collective COVID-19 zeitgeist we distanced awkwardly from our kin, but came a little closer to understanding what is essential.

Quarantining with the objects we've accumulated, many of us took the opportunity to assess each of them anew. We revisited our once indispensable books, appliances, wardrobe items, and souvenirs with a discriminating eye. No thing, we're learning, is truly "indispensable." Everything—ourselves included—has a shelf life. Post-pandemic, will we still trust our compulsion to accumulate material objects? Will we be thus compelled at all?

When I began this book in 2015, I joked with friends that it was "the world's longest suicide note." I mean, why else start giving everything away? Don't worry; that isn't my style. But the steady unloading of stuff has been and will continue to be part of an ongoing process of letting go.

It's not the abstraction it once was. Several times in these pages I've mentioned the medical crisis that befell me in 2018. I wish I could say I'm on a straight path to recovery, but my prognosis is uncertain. It's a reminder that my only essential possession—this challenged but precious body—will make its own decision about how long to stick around. It may be a while. Or not. Who can say?

Whenever the time might come, I'd like to step off the stage as lightly as possible. That will take a few more trips to the curb. Meanwhile, I'll keep telling stories. They are, in the end, the only things with any real value—and the only part of me I really want to leave you with.

Acknowledgments

CREATION

Zena Kruzick
Silvi Alcivar
Colleen Shelley
Laurie Weed
Laurie Wagner
Karen Charmaine Blansfield
Sharyl McGrew
Monica Pasqual
Debra Greenwald
Sandy Pollack
Dana Albany

SUPPORT & INSPIRATION

Sivani Babu
Sabine Bergmann
Amy Bergstein
Marianne Betterly-Kohn
Rob Brezsny
Steven Brock
Laarry Brown
Erin Byrne
Nicole Chase
Susie Davis
Ben Douglas
Carroll Dunham
Perry Garfinkel
Rick Gaynor
Don George
Marsea Goldberg
Roslyn Greenwald-Miller
Larry Habegger
Scott Harrison
Teri Hollowell
James Hopkins
Teri Ketchie
Stephani Lesh
Nancy Lindborg
Jeff Lipsky

Kimberley Lovato
Christine Marie Mason
Elliot Marseille
Ruth McVeigh
Marc Mowrey
Terra Muzick
Kate Nasse
Kristina Nemeth
Dwayne Newton
Wes "Scoop" Nisker
Karen Nuñez
Michael Pedroni
Elaine, Bill & Kathryn Petrocelli
Catherine Porter
D'Arcy Richardson
Mary Roach
Steve Rosenberg
Andrea Schnoor
Lavinia Spalding
Patty Spiglanin
Lisa Tracy
Noe Venable
Nonnie Welch
Karen West
Bonnie Zane

108 BELOVED OBJECTS

All of the objects in this book are intended to be given away to you, the reader. To acquire one of them (and only one per person, please), send me an email stating why you'd like that particular object. I will let you know if it is unclaimed.

If you do accept stewardship of one of these beloved objects, you will be asked to pay only the cost of postage (which will vary object to object).

In asking for an object, you grant me permission to publish your request (anonymously) and your city/country of residence on the 108Objects.com website, as well as on social media.

If one of these objects calls to you, please write me at jeff@jeffgreenwald.com.

www.ingramcontent.com/pod-product-compliance
Lightning Source LLC
Chambersburg PA
CBHW041109070526
44583CB00003B/120